Delighting IN GOD

Prayer Is Opening the Heart to a Friend

KRIS COFFIN STEVENSON

Pacific Press Publishing Association
Boise, Idaho
Oshawa, Ontario, Canada

Edited by Bonnie Tyson-Flyn
Designed by Tim Larson
Cover illustration by Darrel Tank
Typeset in New Century Schoolbook 11/13

Unless otherwise noted, all Scripture quotations are taken from the New International Version.

ISBN 0-8163-1274-5

96 97 98 99 00 • 5 4 3 2 1

Contents

Introduction

I must admit that I balked at the idea of writing a book on prayer. I would much rather write a novel whose enchanting characters and strong story line would so move you that by the end, you would be down on your knees, sobbing and asking God for forgiveness and new direction in your life.

Well, maybe someday. Maybe not.

In any case, when the Spirit began nudging me to write about prayer, I marshaled my counterarguments. First, I might have been imagining the call. Imaginative people can do that easily. So I dragged my feet a bit, trying to convince myself I was just making it up.

When the nudging continued, I raised a new argument: What insights into prayer did I have to offer that hadn't been given before? I received no immediate answer, just a persistent still, small voice.

My next argument seemed solid. I could not claim to be a George Müller or a Billy Graham. That ought to solve the problem right there. But the voice continued to call.

I next tried for absolute proof. I asked for a "sign" that I should write the book. God would have been justified in throwing me into the path of a whale right about then. He didn't give me the sign I asked for but gave the assurance that I didn't need one. The voice was still there.

Finally, the Lord cranked up the volume so there was no mistaking the call. To ignore the voice now would be absolute disobedience. I acquiesced, but there is no merit in being badgered into obedience. I ought to know by now to step a little livelier when I hear the voice.

This material began as a small seed of interest several years ago during a searching period of my life. That seed was watered by materials and books that made their way mysteriously into my possession, as well as the enlightenment of the Holy Spirit. That seed eventually burst into bloom in the form of a Week of Prayer series that was published in *Accent*, a publication of the General Conference of Seventh-day Adventists, Church Ministries Department. They have graciously given permission for that material to be expanded and revised into its present shape.

The experience of writing this manuscript has been filled with incredible moments when it seemed as if the Lord leaned over my shoulder and touched the computer keyboard Himself. I have been awed by how God has coordinated events to fall neatly into place. I have also been humbled to see where I have neglected to learn lessons that I could have passed on to others.

The Lord did distinctly answer one of my arguments—that I didn't know what I had to offer on the subject of prayer. When I sat down to outline my ideas, He showed me immediately that my contribution was to give people tools with which to make prayer work for them. This book doesn't emphasize the philosophical or theological aspects of prayer. Instead, it is an exceedingly practical book, plain and straightforward. But I hope it will show you, step by step, *how* to meet with God, drawing you closer and closer into an intimate relationship with Him, through the practice of tried and true methods.

My prayer is that you will find the concepts clear and easy to practice in daily life, that you will make seeking after God the focus and priority of your existence. This is what the voice called to me; this is what the voice is calling to you.

Chapter 1

A Torrent of Grace

When I was in academy, I decided I needed a boyfriend. This was actually a more pure desire than it might sound. I was a senior and felt as though I needed to experience the fun and camaraderie that a close male friend would provide. I was a little shy and had struggled to play the act-disinterested-and-catch-a-man games. So, I decided to bring in the big guns for backup. I would pray that God would bring me a boyfriend. Now I'm sure God has had many stranger requests in His time than playing matchmaker in the sky. But I boldly went before Him, claiming my favorite text: Psalm 37:4. "Delight yourself in the Lord and he will give you the desires of your heart."

I placed my request before the Lord, believing He would answer it, and claimed my text as proof. I also pointed out all the logical reasons why my request should be granted. I truly believed that I was following biblical principles with the best of motives and that God would answer my trusting prayer.

And so, with butterflies in my stomach, I attended the get-acquainted school picnic at the beginning of the year, waiting to see whom God would pick for me.

Right about now you're probably squirming with embarrassment for me. How naive could I have been? Why would I think God would serve up an eligible bachelor within hours of my heartfelt cry? And just what would happen to my faith when my request went begging?

But by the time the evening activities were over, I had a boyfriend—unsolicited and unpicked by me, a real answer to prayer.

Which brings me to my point: Why pray? Is it to conjure up much-desired needs or wants? Is it a soothing, meditational chant to bring relaxation from a stressful world? Is it a necessary duty that Christians are called to participate in?

The concept of prayer—real, true, gritty, knees-in-the-dirt prayer—frightens most Christians. What exactly does God want them to do? How do they go about it? And, most important, is anybody really listening, or are they just sending signals out into an empty universe? Because of these questions, few sermons are given on prayer, few talks or seminars emphasize the practical aspects of prayer, and few people actively engage in a meaningful prayer life. Lots of people *talk* about prayer; few people actually pray.

Praying is a tough thing, when you think about it. It's the end of the day. You're tired. The kids have been screaming; the boss was cranky; two people were out sick, making your work twice as heavy; the electric bill was three times what you expected; and the VCR just ate a tape. So you flop into bed, and just before you go under, you think, *I gotta pray*. So you drag yourself up into semisitting position, close your eyes, and mumble something about getting a good night's sleep and blessings on your family. When you open your eyes after talking to God, it's morning and you dropped out of the conversation somewhere after "Bless the missionaries and the colporteurs."

But halfhearted blessings for food and half-asleep bedtime prayers are only shadows of what real communication with God is all about. If this kind of prayer leaves you unsatisfied and thirsty for more clear communication with God, He will lead you on a marvelous and unimaginably exciting journey to learn how to delight in Him.

Any heartfelt searching after God, spoken or unspoken, eloquent or simple, is a prayer. To approach the throne of God requires an attitude, a state of mind, not a formula or a magical chant. God wants to be approached. He ignores stumbled beginnings, poor grammar, lack of religious instruction in prayer, previous sins, or present environmental circumstances. He simply wants to maintain the connection so that growth and understanding can take place.

The Bible has been marketed as God's Word to us. But, really, it is only one side of the conversation. To read the Bible without prayer is to listen without responding, a very unnerving form of conversation. The same is true of nature. To enjoy "God's second book" without commenting to Him on the spiritual joy it brings you is to be a very poor conversationalist. True Bible study is always accompanied by prayer, not only prayer for guidance in understanding the Scriptures, but a form of prayer in the reading itself. If a conversation with a friend is composed of both of you talking and responding, then you cannot separate your words to God in prayer and His words to you through the Bible or nature. They are the two sides of a conversation.

The purpose of prayer

Why is prayer important? There is no one good answer. Prayer encompasses so much in a Christian life that its purposes are multiple and vast. The most immediate effect, though, is that it brings you into contact with the Creator of the universe. Establishing this communication leads to a relationship that slowly grows with use over a period of time. In this type of prayer, the process is the end result; the journey itself is the bottom line.

If eating feeds the physical self and talking feeds the relational self, praying is the meat of the spiritual self. A child will not grow without nourishment, and your own body will not be sustained without daily intake of food and water. As you pray, you grow; and as you grow, you learn more fully how to pray so that you continue to grow. The Lord rewards those who seek after Him with added spiritual insight.

Try forming a relationship with someone without talking or communicating in any way. Since Jesus isn't still on earth in His physical and readily conversable form, He provided another way for us to grow in our relationship with Him. It's pretty amazing when you think about it. Anytime, anywhere, you can connect into that spiritual radar and reach up to God.

A lot of the problem with prayer comes from a misunderstanding of the purpose of prayer. Is God just there to bless our food (and the hands that prepared it), to distribute traveling mercies, and to give out bursts of supernatural wisdom during algebra tests? One of the most beautiful passages in the Bible, Matthew 6:25-34, gives a clue.

> I tell you, do not worry about your life, what you will eat or drink; or about your body, what you will wear. Is not life more important than food, and the body more important than clothes? Look at the birds of the air; they do not sow or reap or store away in barns, and yet your heavenly Father feeds them. Are you not much more valuable than they? Who of you by worrying can add a single hour to his life?
>
> And why do you worry about clothes? See how the lilies of the field grow. They do not labor or spin. Yet I tell you that not even Solomon in all his splendor was dressed like one of these. If that is how God clothes the grass of the field, which is here today and tomorrow is thrown into the fire, will he not much more clothe you, O you of little faith? So do not worry, saying, "What shall we eat?" or "What shall we drink?" or "What shall we wear?" For the pagans run after all these things, and your heavenly Father knows that you need them. But seek first his kingdom and his righteousness, and all these things will be given to you as well. Therefore do not worry about tomorrow, for tomorrow will worry about itself. Each day has enough trouble of its own.

The key words in that passage are verse 33: "Seek first his kingdom and his righteousness, and all these things will be given to you as well." How do you seek His kingdom and His righteousness? Through persistent coming to God in prayer. The first responsibility of a Christian is to seek a relationship with God, and then everything else will be taken care of. Without this relationship, people get unrealistic expectations about answers to prayer and wonder whether God is even listening. They're focusing on what God can *do* for them and on what *prayer* can *do* for them instead of focusing on God and their relationship with Him.

Prayer is so widely misused and misunderstood that most of us don't even realize its importance and potential. When I first began to study about prayer, I started looking up some of the scriptural references to prayer. I stumbled upon a text in Samuel that I had previously studied, but I had never noticed exactly what it meant. It's definitely not what you would expect. First Samuel 12:23 says, "As for me, far be it from me that I should *sin* against the Lord by failing to pray for you" (emphasis mine).

In this text, Samuel is addressing the children of Israel just prior to their receiving Saul as king. Although the Israelites had rebelled by going directly against what God had planned for them by asking for a king, Samuel declares that it would be a sin if he should neglect to pray for them!

I was taught that sin is anything that separates a person from God. It is easy to think of sin as an action—such as lying or committing adultery. But this text startled me with the realization that *not* doing something could be a sin as well. That would make neglecting to nurture a relationship with God a sin. In fact, neglect is as great a sin as outright rejection of God because it leads to the same result.

When the Lord convicts you with an understanding of how crucial a role prayer plays in the Christian life, He also extends a blessing with the conviction, "Blessed are those who hunger and thirst for righteousness, for they will be filled" (Matthew 5:6).

Spiritual food

So, if prayer is the basis of our relationship with God, and a lack of prayer is a sinful separation from Him, what, then, does prayer accomplish? If we continue with the analogy of food, prayer is the mealtimes during which we stock up on carbohydrates to give us energy throughout the day. It builds our spiritual muscle and helps us grow. It forms spiritual white blood cells that ward off temptation. If the food we eat eventually becomes part of our very cells, then our prayers eventually become part of our inner selves, the center of our being.

Prayer allows God to work in us and through us. As our relationship with Him grows, His voice becomes clearer, His will more certain in our lives. The entire future of our Christian experience hinges on what goes on between us and God during our prayer times. This is the process of sanctification most readily understood. As we make "hungering and thirsting" after God a priority in our lives, "he who began a good work in you will carry it on to completion until the day of Christ Jesus" (Philippians 1:6).

The seventeenth-century Carmelite monk known as Brother Lawrence lived a life that illustrated in its purest form prayer as the center of the Christian's life. Every act that he did was accompanied by prayer, and he felt that we were much to be pitied that we contented ourselves with so little when God was prepared to give us so much.

> God . . . has infinite treasure to bestow. . . . Blind as we are, we hinder God and stop the current of His graces. But when He finds a soul penetrated with a lively faith, He pours into it His graces and favors plentifully; there they flow like a torrent which, after being forcibly stopped against its ordinary course, when it has found a passage, spreads itself with impetuosity and abundance.[1]

Contrary to popular belief, God *wants* to bless us. In Malachi 3:10, He promises to pour out so many blessings that we don't even have room to receive them. But to approach God, hands outstretched for blessings, without having a relationship upon which to base our requests is to treat Him like a big lottery machine in the sky; cross your fingers and pull the lever—and if you've been nice and not naughty maybe you'll get what you asked for. No one would consider using a friend that way, but we frequently treat God that way.

So why did God answer my prayer and send me a boyfriend? I think God has to reach us where we are. My faith at the time wasn't strong enough to handle any larger truths about God and prayer. That answer to a sincere prayer helped me to realize as a teenager that God did care about me personally, that prayer was a connection with Him, and that it really did work. Later, God would lead me farther into an understanding of prayer and test my faith with His answers to my prayers. But my prayer journey essentially started with that first major answer to prayer, and God has been gently encouraging me on ever since.

If you're just starting out on a prayer journey, or if you want to make a decision right now to begin a relationship with God, He stands waiting to lead you on.

> If we come to God, feeling helpless and dependent, as we really are, and in humble, trusting faith make known our wants to Him whose knowledge is infinite . . . , He can and will attend to our cry, and will let light shine into our hearts. Through sincere prayer we are brought into connection with the mind of the Infinite.[2]

Since that day when I claimed Psalm 37:4 ("Delight yourself in the Lord and he will give you the desires of your heart") as my favorite text, I've learned a great deal. That text is still my favorite, but the focus has now changed from the "desire of your heart" to "delight in the Lord." There is great delight in learning to talk a God who stands waiting to pour out a "torrent of grace" in your life.

Prayer: God , give me the courage to be willing to start a prayer life. Please come and be the tour guide in my prayer journal.

Practice: Memorize Matthew 6:33, 34.

---

1. Brother Lawrence, *The Practice of the Presence of God* (New York: Fleming H. Revell, 1895), 43.
2. Ellen G. White, *Steps to Christ* (Hagerstown, Md.: Review and Herald, 1908), 97.

Chapter 2

Consider It All Joy

Are you convinced that you should make prayer a priority in your life? If so, good. But here's a warning. *All the conviction in the world won't matter a bit if you're not willing to change.* This is where the subject of prayer can get mighty painful. Now you have to contemplate kneeling before an all-knowing God and actually *admitting* that you have sins and problems. And, even worse, allowing Him to examine all the jealously guarded secrets of your life. That's why people usually talk more about prayer than actually pray. It's a humbling and vulnerable position for someone bred to "have it all together" and to always be in control.

Maybe the thought of kneeling down right now and asking God into your life with total security clearance into every aspect may leave you a little squeamish. Well, there's good news: God accepts you where you are and leads you on from there. And to make things easier, He even provides the desire. That's a bonus many Christians often refuse to accept. They think they have to patch up the tattered pieces of their lives *before* they come into God's presence and work up some sort of holy, amenable feeling before they approach the throne of grace. They need to be reminded that it isn't called "grace" for nothing. Jesus says, "My grace is sufficient for you," and He was talking to everyone.

Perhaps you know in your heart that Jesus is calling you, asking you into a prayer fellowship with Him, but that stubborn streak deep inside is saying, "Not now. Maybe next week. Maybe when I've been studying my Bible-study lesson more regularly, I'll be more ready, and I'll feel like turning myself over to God." This is the time to take hold of the grace extended to you and pray this prayer: "Lord, give me the *desire* to actually *want* You in my life." Does that sound blasphemous? But don't you think God would rather you prayed that prayer than wait until you think you're ready?

It doesn't matter whether every fiber in your body rebels against the idea of praying that prayer. It doesn't matter whether you say it between clenched teeth. It doesn't matter whether you aren't sure you totally mean it. Because you know what? God answers that prayer—He really does. You can never be good enough for God—only willing enough for God.

When the Spirit moves over your troubled heart and breathes rest and peace into the turmoil, the resistance will melt away to be replaced by a true desire to know God better, to understand His mysterious ways, and to be a part of His fellowship. But it is not a natural act to want God in that way. Our sinful human natures lust after the immediate pleasurable gratifications of our society and scorn the quiet inner workings of the Spirit. You must invite God into your life to start making changes—He will not come in uninvited. But He will provide even the desire for Him to help you begin the incredible journey.

Preparation

But there *is* work that you must do in preparation. Once the Lord has given you the wonderful gift of desire, before you can move on to the greater truths that He stands waiting to reveal to you, you must prepare your heart. First John 1:9 says, "If we confess our sins, he is faithful and just and will forgive us our sins and purify us from all unrighteousness." And verse 10: "If we claim we have not sinned, we make him out to be a liar and his word has no place in our lives."

It is easy to excuse away sins only before you contemplate the incredible sacrifice made by both God and His Son to make right those petty sins we guard so anxiously.

The centre of salvation is the Cross of Jesus, and the reason it is so easy to obtain salvation is because it cost

God so much. The Cross is the point where God and sinful man merge with a crash and the way to life is opened—but the crash is on the heart of God.[1]

With a truly repentant heart and an accurate knowledge of the fact we are sinners and are saved only through His intercession, our hearts can be cleansed and made ready for Him to move in. As He forgives our relational barriers to Him, we also must forgive those who have damaged their relationships with us. The Lord's Prayer says, "Forgive us our debts, as we also have forgiven our debtors" (Matthew 6:12).

But as we move along on our prayer journey, the depths of our human nature will continually be revealed to us by the Holy Spirit. If we resist at any point, the spiritual journey has to be halted until the troublesome point is cleared up. This is why so many Christians never seem to progress. Once they hit upon a snag in their lives, they spend the rest of the time making excuses, rationalizing, and comparing themselves to other Christians. If the Holy Spirit is convicting you on a certain point, even if it seems to be minor and no one else is paying the slightest attention to it—DON'T ARGUE. Oswald Chambers says in his devotional book *My Utmost for His Highest*, "Whenever there is doubt, quit immediately, no matter what it is. Nothing is a mere detail."[2]

I discovered this quite dramatically when I first began my prayer journey. For almost two years, I had been feeling as if the Holy Spirit was urging me to give up TV. But I had dozens of rationalizations for not doing it. After all, most "good" Christians have TV. I was not a TV junkie (I thought). I didn't watch all day, and I was careful not to watch violent and unhealthy programming. But yet there continued to be that persistent urging. At one point I actually acquiesced. I had the cable turned off in the apartment while I was gone for the summer, effectively ruining our reception. But when I got back, it was too easy to be talked back into turning it on by a friend who depended on my TV for entertainment. She even offered to split the cost of reconnecting the cable. I gave in, and it was another year before I finally made the break again.

But after I did, the Lord blessed me with a tremendous outpouring of spiritual insight and spiritual growth. In just a few short months, I grew faster and farther than I had in years. What I really learned from that experience was that when you're convicted—listen and act! God reaches down and touches you in areas where you do pay attention. For another person, TV might never be a problem in their lives, but materialism has become his or her god. Or sports or looks or success. Relational blocks with God come in all varieties and are specific to each person. That's why when the Spirit highlights something in your life, no matter how extreme or silly it might seem, trust God to know what He's doing—and *give it up*. Does it make any sense to reject God's blessing for a particular genre of books you read or the type of clothes you wear or the number of hours you work? If you are truly serious about pursuing a relationship with God, there will be sacrifices and costs on your side. It's one thing to say, "God, forgive my sins, and give me a clean heart." It's another thing to turn off the TV or give away those tickets you stood in line to get or put down that book you're reading in order to come to God with a clear conscience, ready to receive the multifaceted blessings He is waiting to place in your hands.

The Comforter

Jesus gives a detailed description in John 16:5-15 of the Holy Spirit's job. In this passage the Spirit is called the *Comforter* in the King James Version, *Counselor* in the New International Version, and *Advocate* in the Jerusalem Bible. Jesus says that He is going away; and the Counselor will come to convict the world in regard to sin, righteousness, and the judgment. In verse 13 the "Spirit of truth" speaks from Jesus and guides in truth and tells what is yet to come.

The Spirit is Jesus' way of personally being with everyone, of tailoring a "Christian growth program" for each individual, mindful of their own strengths, weaknesses, and abilities. Notice that the Spirit convicts, not just about sin, but also about righteousness. Through the Spirit's ministrations, we not only are shown where we need to let go and let God into our lives, but also receive the spiritual gifts God is prepared to give us.

As you start on a prayer journey, it is imperative that you pray for the Spirit to guide you. Unfortunately, this concept has been distorted with the New Age teaching of spirit guides. The Spirit sent from God *is* God, is part of the Trinity, and is privy to the highest heavenly secrets. When you pray for the Holy Spirit, it's *God* who is right there with you. Jesus says, "All that belongs to the Father is mine. That is why I said the Spirit will take from what is mine and make it known to you" (John 16:15).

The Spirit's voice is so quiet that we sometimes strain to hear it. But its very softness requires us to clear out the clutter that blocks God's influence in our lives. If we continue to follow the Spirit's beckoning call, obediently and without question, He will navigate us through the confusion of this world. The clearer we hear His call, the more power will transform our lives, but always we must make following His call our focus.

Not only should we pray that the Spirit will breathe new breath into our sin-choked lives, but we should also pray that the Spirit will move over the troubled lives of friends and relations who may need His prodding to begin their own journey. Because the Spirit does not come unasked into a life, we sometimes need to do the asking for a friend.

The Spirit also brings wisdom to our spiritual journey, an essential quality in sorting through the confusing melee of theologies today. Everyone has probably imagined what he or she would do if visited by a genie granting three wishes. I, too, wanted to ask for three more wishes. But 1 Kings 3:5 tells how Solomon *actually* gets that chance! God comes to him and says, "Ask for whatever you want Me to give you." What a chance! Now's the time to ask for that new car, that new house, or, if you're feeling a bit righteous, world peace. But what does Solomon ask for? Wisdom, or more accurately, a discerning heart to distinguish between right and wrong. What does he get? A discerning heart, plus a new car, a new house, and world peace.

In praying for wisdom and guidance as brought by the Spirit, we are praying to be able to distinguish between right and wrong in a world where choices seem increasingly gray. When the path ahead seems unclear and the road to destruction lies so close by, with prayer as our anchor, we can step forward in faith that we will find the right path. Our faith will also keep us steady when it seems as if we are the only ones using that path.

Facts, not feelings

A funny thing happens after you've had a really high spiritual experience. You've heard a great sermon or read an inspiring book or attended an invigorating seminar, and you come home basking in the glory of the Lord. You bubble over with excitement and can't wait to tell everyone what's happened to you. You wonder why you've had such a problem conquering a certain sin, because now indulging that sin seems so petty compared to the eternal. But then what happens? Maybe a day later, maybe three or four days, maybe a week, maybe even a month, suddenly all that wonderful feeling is gone. It has evaporated, gone without a trace, and you're left feeling discouraged and depressed, wondering if you imagined all those spiritual insights.

So, what's the problem with God? Where did He go? Why did He drop you in the dust just when things were getting good? It's typical that we would blame God for the problem. What we have to learn is that God and our spiritual experience are totally independent of human feeling. Paul says in Hebrews 11:1, "Now faith is being sure of what we hope for and certain of what we do not see." It is faith that holds you steady when you feel sick, tired, and discouraged and you doubt the leading of God. "We have to learn to live in the grey day according to what we saw on the mount."[3]

There will be times of great spiritual height in your life—mountaintop experiences. But while we are on this earth, God calls us to minister in the valleys, refreshed and sustained by our visits to the mountain. Even during the spiritually low times, be assured that God does not change, does not walk away from you, does not ignore the pain you are going through as you fight despondency.

Jesus, our example, had a dramatic mountaintop experience when He was transfigured with Moses and Elijah and appeared before the terrified disciples. Although Peter suggested that they put up booths there on the mountain, Jesus led His disciples down from the mountain to continue ministering to the people (see Matthew 17:1-9; Mark 9:1-8).

Moses was angry when, after his mountaintop experience on Mt. Sinai, where he was allowed a glimpse of God, he came down off the mountain to find his people cavorting with sin (see Ezekiel 32:19, 20).

In these instances, and others, those who have communed with God on the mountain have returned to the valleys and have had to continue by faith in the work set before them while they were with God.

If you are waiting for undeniable proof that there is a God and that He wants you to get to know Him better, you will never find it. But God speaks to everyone personally, and in His speaking to you, you will find enough "proof" to continue on your journey.

In John 1:47-50, Philip brings Nathanael to see Jesus. To Nathanael's astonishment, Jesus says upon meeting him, " 'Here is a true Israelite, in whom there is nothing false.' 'How do you know me?' Nathanael asked. Jesus answered, 'I saw you while you were still under the fig tree before Philip called you.' Then Nathanael declared, 'Rabbi, you are the Son of God; you are the King of Israel.' "

In everyone's life there comes a Nathanael experience, a time when the Lord obviously and supernaturally reaches out and impacts your life in such a way as to leave no doubt of His existence and His intentions. It is a humbling and awe-inspiring moment when you realize that the Lord of the universe has seen you "under the fig tree." Often a Nathanael experience happens when a person first gives his or her life to God. But it can also happen at the beginning of a spiritual journey. It is a moment when God gives proof of His love and His personal concern.

My Nathanael experience was my prayer of faith at the beginning of my senior year in high school—that God would find me a boyfriend. I had been raised a Christian, but I was now old enough to really begin a mature Christian walk with God, to grow in knowledge and understanding of His infinite wisdom and grace. This significant and incredible answer to prayer, a benevolent act from a loving Father, was my own personal and undeniable proof that there was a God and that He cared about me. That answer to prayer was a blessing throughout the entire relationship, which, although it did not end in marriage, was what I had hoped it would be and was also a wonderful growing experience and preparation for marriage at a future date.

"There is greater encouragement for us in the least blessing we ourselves receive from God than in all the accounts we can read of the faith and experience of others."[4] The only problem with Nathanael experiences is that you tend to forget them so quickly and start questioning all over again. Sometimes God graciously repeats a Nathanael experience to strengthen a wobbly faith. It is always wonderful confirmation to receive new evidence of God's love. But it really shouldn't be necessary in a Christian's life. God wants us to grow beyond needing to repeatedly prove His existence. He wants us to trust Him when prayers aren't answered with a Yes, when new proof is withheld, when everything seems against us. That is the faith Paul talks about, the faith that believes in things not seen—and not felt.

Many years later, after I was married, the Lord answered a tiny, seemingly insignificant prayer, gave my still-wavering faith a boost. Both my husband and I had come down with severe stomach flu. If you've ever had it, you know that while you're in the throes of it, you'd almost rather be dead. I had been up all night, staying close to the toilet. My husband had finally fallen asleep, but I could not find any relief for my misery. No position would ease the nausea, and I was feeling weaker and weaker and more and more frantic.

Finally, I felt I had reached the limit of my endurance, and I prayed (yes, it took me all night to think of it). I asked God to give me just a little bit of sleep so that I would have the strength to endure the agony. The next thing I knew, I was waking up a couple hours later. I had fallen asleep almost immediately at the end of my prayer. That small, but significant answer to prayer when I needed it desperately was like a beacon of light to my spiritual soul, which was grappling at the time with issues of faith.

The Lord is gracious to us all and willing to do what is necessary to help us discover Him, even when we flunk the grade and have to repeat it.

Perseverance

Have you ever heard someone say, "Give your heart to Jesus, and He'll do the rest"? Do you agree with that statement? I don't! From a theological point of view, yes, God "saves" us the moment we ask Him into our lives, and it is God who gives us the power to make changes in our lives. But what that statement implies is that walking the spiritual journey with Christ is easy. Don't let anyone kid you. It's not. Jesus says, "Take up [your] cross and follow me" (Mark 8:34).

Justification is the easiest thing in the world. But sanctification is the hardest thing in the world. Justification is the point where you receive eternal life, where you ask Jesus into your life and He covers you with His righteousness. All that it takes is an invitation on your part, and it's over in a moment. But sanctification is a *process* that continues all your life. It is a long and sometimes arduous journey in which the Lord leads you through various situations to strengthen your faith and make you solid for Him.

That's why, as you consider your spiritual prayer journey, you need to be aware of the grit and determination on your part that need to accompany it. Your decision to get better acquainted with God through prayer will have to be repeated again and again— even when you don't feel like it or your personal environment is somehow not conducive to God searching or it just plain seems fruitless. It means that when you feel overwhelmed or discouraged, you straighten your shoulders and say, "I'm not going to give up. I'm not going to let this thing go."

Where did God go? I wondered after my initial foray into the prayer experience. I was still doing all the "right" things, it seemed, but the feeling I had of closeness with the Father was gone. That was the key, but it took me awhile to see it. God hadn't gone anywhere. He was still right there. What made me think that He was farther away was that I didn't feel as if He was still there. In His infinite wisdom, He wanted to teach me that His promise to "never leave me nor forsake me" wasn't conditional on my feelings; whether I was overjoyed or despondent, He didn't change.

The time during which I was studying about prayer was one of the most personally difficult times of my life. I was besieged by doubts and troubles, depression and futility.

I needed to learn that even if all the external factors in my life seemed to show that God did not exist or, at the very least, did not care about *me*, I could still hang onto my faith and believe He was there.

It may also be that God wants to see just how willing we are to pursue Him. Lots of things in our lives can take up more time, money, and energy than being with God. Some are good, wholesome things like biking or stamp collecting or volunteering at a soup kitchen.

But whatever your hobby or interest, if you compare the time spent pursuing it with the time you spend pursuing God, it can leave you stunned. It's all too easy to give up when spiritual truths don't fall like ripe apples into our lives. But why should we expect to be spoon-fed? Isn't half the fun of an activity the challenge of pursuit? What would dating be without it?

Why shouldn't it be the same with God? A God easily captured, who spills all the secrets of His domain into our unappreciative hands, would soon be a God we would take for granted, grow tired of, and discard.

If you struggle to learn how to master multiplying fractions or save your money for months to buy a new, paid-for camcorder or faithfully practice your oboe every day for an hour so you can become good enough to join the orchestra, aren't these accomplishments infinitely more precious to you for all the effort you put into them?

God, after all, is God. For all His approachableness, He is still a God of mystery and awe, deserving of reverence and worship. Every precious nugget of wisdom wrested out of the dark night of our struggles to find Him will be that much more valuable for the effort. The night Jacob spent wrestling with God produced a blessing far greater than even he could imagine.

Feelings may come and go, but our God is constant. A soul searching for God will only grow stronger on account of the search and will appreciate the treasure that much more when it is found. "Then you will call upon me and come and pray to me, and I will listen to you. You will seek me and find me when you seek me with all your heart" (Jeremiah 29:12, 13).

So don't let discouragement seize you if your high spiritual feelings seem to ebb away and your praise turns to plodding and pleading. In fact, we're told to find joy in the trials and struggles that come our way, for it is through these that we grow and mature. "Consider it pure joy, my brothers, whenever you face trials of many kinds, because you know that the testing of your faith develops perseverance. Perseverance must finish its work so that you may be mature and complete, not lacking anything" (James 1:2-4).

Prayer: As I journey, Lord, give me perseverance to keep pursuing You, even when I feel discouraged or distant from You.

Practice: Write down the *one* thing that you feel is standing in the way of a more satisfying relationship with God. List the reasons you don't want to give it up. What will help you take that next step toward God?

---

1. Oswald Chambers, *My Utmost for His Highest* (Uhrichsville, Ohio: Barbour and Co., Inc., 1963), 70.
2. Ibid., 76.
3. Ibid., 77.
4. Ellen G. White, *The Desire of Ages* (Boise, Idaho: Pacific Press, 1940), 384.

Chapter 3

Still Life

Just a few verses below my favorite text in Psalm 37, I stumbled upon another text that literally gave me pause. "Be still before the Lord and wait patiently for him" (verse 7). I could understand being patient, no matter how much I disliked the concept, but what exactly did it mean to "be still"? My spiritual training had prepared me to memorize Bible verses before the Lord, read the Bible through in a year before the Lord, study the Sabbath School lesson every day before the Lord, but certainly not to "be still before the Lord."

To me, being still equated with being lazy and, viewed kindly, as nonproductive. So as my prayer journey progressed, I began to try to understand just exactly what "being still" encompassed. I wonder if God sometimes watches all our frenetic rushing around and wishes we would just be still for a few minutes. The image comes to mind of our dog-trainer friend, whose beautiful Australian sheep dog kept dancing around the yard in excitement when we came to visit. The trainer finally gave the command to "settle," and the dog obediently crouched down in one spot, still wiggling all over.

After all, it's hard to talk to someone who won't "be still." Have you ever had a conversation with someone like that? You're trying to talk about something important, and his or her eyes keep darting to something more interesting behind you or they keep getting up and adjusting the papers on their desk or putting away the dishes or doing some other distracting activity. I've met a few people like that, and I've wanted to say to them, "Just 'settle,' will you?"

We expect the Lord to come to us preceded by a marching band and with skywriters darting overhead. But as the prophet Elijah found out, the Lord came in a gentle whisper. You have to be pretty still to hear a gentle whisper, especially in today's society, where "perfectly quiet" means you can still hear the refrigerator, the air conditioner, and the traffic on I-5 outside.

So, how do you find the still, small voice? How do you tune in to a frequency jammed by TV, radio, and satellite?

The Daily

When God, through Moses, instituted the tabernacle and its services, two of the focal points were the morning and evening sacrifices—called "The Daily" (see Numbers 28:1-8). Those daily sacrifices are a model of what our devotional lives should be like. First and foremost, we must approach God every day, asking for forgiveness of sins and empowerment to go forward.

Nothing will be accomplished in your prayer life if you pray only on Sabbaths or twice a week or when you feel like it. By asking God into your life every day and spending time with Him, you are giving Him permission to work with you throughout the day.

> Each morning consecrate yourself to God for that day. Surrender all your plans to Him, to be carried out or given up as His providence shall indicate. Thus day by day you may be giving your life into the hands of God, and thus your life will be molded more and more after the life of Christ.[1]

By determining to meet with God every day, you set the stage for regular growth in your prayer life, for an appointment that you keep for the purpose of hearing that still voice, for a time of renewal and pure joy.

It should be as much a part of your routine as rising, eating, and sleeping. If you spend that kind of time with God every day, you can't help but begin to change to be like Him; the Light of the world will eventually illuminate all your plans and ideas. As you grow to understand God's will more perfectly, you will see whether your plans fit with God's plans and ideas for you.

Choosing the best time

After vowing to pray daily, begin looking for the best time and place. Everyone's routine is different, and everyone concentrates better at different times of the day.

Morning is the most common choice of time to spend with God because it gives such a great start to the day. Before anything can mar the day's perfection, before any irritations can trouble your mind, you can sit down with God and get strength, confidence, and instructions for the day.

Meeting with God in the morning also ensures that you make the time to be with Him. In case emergencies or unexpected schedule changes occur later, your prayer time will not be disturbed. Mornings are often quieter than other times. If you're up early enough, you can beat the traffic noise, the phone, and the neighbor's dog.

But mornings also have their drawbacks. For those who have to be at work early with an hour's commute, make lunches, find lost shoes, serve breakfast and clean up, and drop off the kids at school (not to mention getting ready yourself), getting up at 3:00 a.m. to beat the rush might not sound so great!

Your major prayer time needs to be when you can have the most alert and quiet time available. For some people, that might be a lunch hour in which they can close the door to their office or find a nearby park or picnic area to have uninterrupted time. For someone else, the perfect time is right after the kids have been packed out the door for school. For still another, evenings are perfect, when the kids are in bed or a spouse hasn't yet come home from work. The point is, find the best time, schedule it, and keep the appointment.

In fact, consider your prayer time as if it were any other appointment that you would schedule. Write it down on a calendar or appointment book. Treat it with all the importance you would give your best customer, a hot date, or a visit with the boss.

At one time, because I was working at home, I found the best prayer time was in the morning after breakfast when my husband had gone to work. Now that I have a child, I reserve time in the evenings after she's asleep.

The Bible tells us it was Daniel's habit to pray three times a day, morning, noon, and night (see Daniel 6:10). Jesus often spent all day in ministry and would use the night hours for recharging.

If you don't have your major prayer time in the morning, make sure you have time for at least a short worship in the morning. You need to start the day by inviting God into your life so that He is a partner with you in all the day's activities. It's important to start each day prepared so that you don't rush into things without protection.

At the other end, if your major prayer time is not in the evening, make sure you still set aside time to close the day with prayer, asking for forgiveness of sins and turning the day's triumphs and despairs over to God.

Setting the length of time

In her book *Releasing God's Power*, Becky Tirabassi tells of her incredible experience with prayer. She grew up the child of an alcoholic and during her teen years became an alcoholic herself. But then she was introduced to Jesus Christ and started a new walk with Him. Eventually, she married a minister and became actively involved in youth ministry. But something was missing; some of the sparkle had gone out of her Christian experience. On the outside, she kept up a continual round of activities for God, but on the inside, the foundation had collapsed.

Then she and her husband were invited to attend a convention. Although it was not a conference about prayer, every speaker reinforced the idea that without prayer, the Christian is powerless; that prayerlessness is a sin. By the end of the last seminar, Becky sat listening with tears streaming down her face as she realized her need of prayer. She says:

> I was indeed convinced that prayerlessness in the life of *this* believer was sin. If I truly believed that spending

time with God in prayer was actually engaging in conversation with my Creator, Friend, Savior, Leader, and King, *why* would I overlook, avoid, forget, or fall asleep in the middle of prayers?[2]

Her answer was to promise before God and a human witness that she would spend one hour every day in prayer for the rest of her life. Aghast at this seemingly rash promise that she had made, she determined to go ahead with it even if it was "boring." But a surprising thing happened. Instead of being boring, her prayer time became the highlight of her day—an event that she looked forward to with great anticipation.

As she kept that sacred appointment with God, He used the time to clear her life of unhelpful habits, spur her to prioritize her time, and infuse her entire life with discipline. She began to wonder how she had lived without that hour of prayer! Now, more than six years later, Becky has experienced the incredible effect of prayer power in her life. Not only has prayer made revitalizing changes in her own life, it has reached out through her to touch the lives of many, many people, some through incredible answers to prayer. She says, "I am convinced that the practice of prayer in a believer's life is an incredible, virtually untapped power source."[3]

Becky's contract to pray one hour every day is a vivid example of setting aside a certain *amount* of time to pray every day. Maybe that sounds overwhelming to you; maybe it doesn't sound like enough time. Either way, here's something to think about. Spending time with God doesn't decrease the amount of time you have left in the day. Yes, I realize that twenty-four hours in a day, minus one hour of prayer, leaves only twenty-three hours. But who invented time, anyway? The miraculous thing is, the more time you spend with God, the more productive you are as a result. So don't be afraid to challenge yourself and God by setting aside some significant time with Him.

What I discovered while speaking to a women's prayer brunch was that most of the women were amazed at the thought of praying for a half-hour or longer. But it helps to put things in perspective. How long do you spend eating every day? Commuting? Chatting with friends? Daydreaming? Pursuing a sport or a hobby? Watching TV? What things can you shorten or eliminate in order to get the time that you need?

Think of the time you decide to set aside for prayer as a challenge. If you clear time on your schedule, God will teach you how to use it. You don't have to go into your prayer time knowing exactly what you're going to do with it; all you need to know is that you have a God who will meet you there.

Whatever length of time you decide on, try to stick with it. If you think to yourself, *I'll try to pray approximately one hour*, you may find your time shrinking to fifty minutes or forty-five minutes. It helps to set an alarm to go off when your time is over. That way you don't have to think about the time. Certainly you can go over your allotted time if it's possible, but until the alarm goes off, you are free to concentrate entirely on God.

Setting a designated length of time gives you mental freedom in prayer. It means you are not worried about rushing through your prayer so that you can get on to the next thing. It means you don't feel like you have to read a whole chapter of the Bible or any other designated amount of material before you are through with worship. Instead, it gives you the opportunity to focus entirely on what you are doing without being aware of the passage of time. When the alarm goes off, you will actually be surprised at how quickly the time has passed.

The right environment

In order to make your prayer time productive, create for yourself the best environment possible. It's good to set up a permanent spot, one where you can easily form a habit and where you will feel comfortable.

Matthew 6:6 says, "When you pray, go into your room, close the door and pray to your Father." Find a place that you can use regularly. It might be a spare bedroom, a study, the kitchen table, a special spot outdoors like a porch or garden, or even, like the Bible mentions, a closet where you can be uninterrupted. It doesn't need to be perfect; it just needs to be big enough for you and God.

If there are too many distractions at home, look elsewhere for your prayer spot. In warmer climates, you might be able to use a park or other spot outdoors. Or you might be able to have privacy at work in an office or meeting room. Also try using a study carrel in the library or a church (it doesn't have to be your own if it is convenient and open). The main thing is to find a place where you can concentrate and totally devote your thoughts to God.

In his book *Too Busy Not to Pray*, Pastor Bill Hybels describes the need for a special place to pray and tells how he set up his own spot. He talks about how couples have a special, romantic place they go on nights out that is "theirs" and how families often vacation in the same spot, in a place that feels like a "second home."

> I created such a prayer room near the credenza in a corner of my former office. In my prayer place I put an open Bible, a sign that says "God is able," a crown of thorns to remind me of the suffering Savior and a shepherd's staff that I often hold up while making requests.
>
> That office corner became a holy place for me. I arrived there around six o'clock in the morning when no one was around and the phone was unlikely to ring, and there I communed with the Lord. I poured out my heart to him, worshiped him, prayed for members of my congregation and received remarkable answers to prayer.[4]

Furnishing your prayer spot with objects that turn your thoughts toward God is helpful. You might use your Bible, a special picture of Jesus or other devotional picture, a flower arrangement, or even fresh flowers in season. Have other devotional books, paper, and pencil handy for use during your prayer time. I always gravitated toward a certain comfy chair, and soon all my books and papers were piled nearby for easy access. You want to make your spot as appealing as possible so that you will *want* to go there and so you will be blessed and calmed by being in that place.

It is wonderful when you have the opportunity to approach God the Creator outdoors in nature. Whether you are able to be with God outside or to view His creation through a window or even a picture, you can always "go into the fields with Christ" in your heart.

> During [Jesus'] ministry He loved to gather the people about Him under the blue heavens, on some grassy hillside, or on the beach beside the lake. Here, surrounded by the works of His own creation, He could turn the thoughts of His hearers from the artificial to the natural. . . . So it is with all who go into the fields with Christ in their hearts. They will feel themselves surrounded with a holy influence. . . . By communion with God in nature, the mind is uplifted, and the heart finds rest.[5]

Try to eliminate all possible distractions. That means letting the answering machine answer the phone—or taking it off the hook altogether. It means not answering the doorbell or watching out the window to see what the neighbors are doing. It means the TV is off, the computer is off, the stove is off, the iron is off, the beeper is off, and the radio is off. It means the late correspondence is put on hold, the dirty dishes are forgotten, tomorrow's midterm is temporarily ignored, and the coming weekend's schedule is not a priority.

Distractions also fall outside the realm of things you can directly control, like the Off button on an appliance. People are usually the biggest distraction and the hardest to contain. That's why early-morning and late-evening hours are good because fewer people distractions are around.

You may have to "retrain" the people nearest you in order to get the privacy you desire. For a spouse, try to explain that during this time you cannot be disturbed unless an emergency the size of a brontosaurus attacks your house. If a spouse wants to join you, set up another time when you can have worship together, but preserve your own private prayer time. You need to personally charge your own batteries and allow God to talk to you individually.

For very young children, it is better to find a time when they are asleep or out of the house. They will not understand why you don't want them around. Explain to older children why you want to have quiet time with God. Of course, be sure to have worship with them, as well. And don't be upset if your children see you praying. It is good for them to see an adult, especially a parent, making God a priority. They will remember that kind of modeling.

A boss or secretary may be harder to explain to. Make sure your prayer time is not perceived as interfering with your job. If you use a lunch hour, keep in mind Matthew 6:5, 6, which recommends praying in private. You don't want co-workers feeling you are a "Holy Joe." On the other hand, it isn't necessary to be secretive about what you are doing. A simple explanation like, "I use part of my lunch hour as a time of personal devotions with God," should be understood by just about everyone. Coming into work early before any-one else is there might be another way to get quiet time without distractions.

There will always be interruptions at some time or other that cannot be avoided. In the book *The Musician's Quest*, author George MacDonald describes a devout man in the village who erupts into an angry tirade when interrupted at his prayers. His long hours of devotion were sadly negated by that angry outburst. If interruptions do occur, try to handle them gra-ciously but firmly. After all, your Christian witness may be rather tarnished if you yell at someone for disturbing your prayer time.

Above all, persevere

Hebrews 10:36 says, "You need to persevere so that when you

have done the will of God, you will receive what he has promised." God is willing and waiting to make great changes in your life if you make the time for Him every day. Sometimes it may seem that the last thing you want to do is get up early and talk to God. But stick with it. Even when it seems you're not accomplishing anything, be patient. God is working with you. He's disciplining you and hardening your spiritual muscles so that you will be strong for Him.

There is a reward for your faithfulness. "Blessed is the man who perseveres under trial, because when he has stood the test, he will receive the crown of life that God has promised to those who love him" (James 1:12).

We are all human, and humans make mistakes. If you skip a day or a week or a month with God, don't let the guilt keep you from returning to Him. Ask for His power to make you faithful. Sometimes all you can do is pray for the *desire* to pray. God will answer even that simple prayer. Brother Lawrence describes returning to God after an absence this way:

> When sometimes he had not thought of God for a good while, he did not disquiet himself for it; but, after having acknowledged his wretchedness to God, he returned to Him with so much the greater trust in Him as he had found himself wretched through forgetting Him.[6]

Take the challenge that God has set before you—to find Him through your own daily scheduled prayer time. Give Him the opportunity of doing an incredible work in your life. Let Him change you from prayer-less to prayer-ful, from prayer wimp to prayer warrior.

Prayer: In my hectic rushed, rushed life, give me perspective to put You first God, to make all my other priorities revolve around You.

Practice: Draw up your own personal prayer contract. List when, where, how long, and how often you will pray. Schedule it into your appointment book.

---

1. Ellen G. White, *Steps to Christ*, 70.
2. Becky Tirabassi, *Releasing God's Power* (Nashville, Tenn.: Thomas Nelson, 1990), 31.
3. Ibid., 9.
4. Bill Hybels, *Too Busy Not to Pray* (Downers Grove, Ill.: InterVarsity Press, 1988), 42.
5. Ellen G. White, *The Desire of Ages*, 291.
6. Brother Lawrence, *The Practice of the Presence of God*, 21.

Chapter 4

Dream Stream

When I was twelve, I spent a delightful summer with my father doing research in the mountains of the western United States. At one point it was necessary for us to take a three-day hike up into the mountains. After we had packed everything we thought we'd need into our backpacks, we set out on the trail.

At the beginning of the journey, we looked with dismay on the wide, tumbling river that we had to cross. The current was swift, and we were in danger of being swept downstream. So, instead of crossing immediately, we began to follow the river upstream, in the direction we wanted to head.

The hike was arduous. The path—if it could be called a path—wound steadily upward. Sometimes it disappeared into a marshy area that we had to cautiously circumvent. Often it was criss-crossed with fallen logs that we clambered over and under. And still the terrain grew steeper. My pack began to feel twice as heavy, the straps cut deeply into my shoulders, and blisters began forming on my heels.

As the air became thinner, my breath came in gasps, and I could hike only a few yards before I had to stop and rest. It seemed we would never reach our destination. Many times, after resting for a moment on a fallen log, I could hardly muster the energy and courage to get up and keep going forward.

Doggedly I followed my father, watching the backs of his boots as we went on, step by step. Often my father would stop to readjust my pack or transfer some of its contents to his much-heavier pack. Sometimes he had to give me a hand to scramble up a steep spot or shout encouragement as I shakily crossed a ravine on a fallen log.

I wanted to suggest stopping and camping for the evening, but I knew that my father had a safe and ideal camping spot already picked out. Finally, more weary than I had ever thought I could be, I stumbled into our campsite.

After our tent was set up and supper was bubbling over the fire, I began to explore our surroundings. The scenery was breathtaking; the view was incredible. From up there you could see to eternity. Next to our campsite ran a sparkling mountain stream, icy cold, straight from a glacier. I played around it, jumping back and forth from bank to bank and testing how long I could leave my bare feet in its frigid waters.

"That," my father said, to my astonishment, "is the same raging river we were afraid to cross in the valley."

In my prayer analogy, that torrential river is like the gulf many see between themselves and God. Into the river run all their preconceived ideas about God they have grown up with and all the seemingly insurmountable problems in their lives. It seems completely impossible to cross that flood, to make any progress against the rushing current of things that separate them from God: illness, grief, money, failure, time, peer pressure, bills, TV, doubts, past experience, materialism, fears, death, relationships.

But then, our Father says, "Come, follow Me." And He leads us up through the canyon, steadying us as we slip, giving us a hand when we are weak, taking our burdens upon Himself—and always leading us higher.

Prayer is that hike. It's the journey we take when we set out to get to know God. It's the course we follow in dealing with insurmountable problems. We steadily follow Him onward, trusting His judgment and the course that He picks. We will labor long and hard, get blisters on our knees, and feel the heavy burden of sin cutting deep into our shoulders. We may wish to stop, ache to turn and run back into the ease of the valley. But eventually we'll look back down the canyon and see how high we've climbed, how far we can see, how incredible is the view. And there in front of us, instead of a life-threatening problem or an impossible distance between us and God, is a picturesque alpine stream—a simple solution to our problem, a clear view of the situation, a trial-forged relationship with God. And our Father will be right there with us, inviting us to "sup with Him."

If prayer is the journey, then we ought to discover the best and most efficient methods of traveling. If we've determined to spend time praying every day, then we need to know how to use the time we've set aside, how best to take advantage of those precious minutes with God.

The idea of praying for an hour or even half an hour is daunting to many people. It is helpful to know what components can be included in this prayer time and how to break prayer down into more easily definable sections.

Using the Bible

You might wonder just where Bible study fits into prayer time. Should an hour of "prayer time" be used solely for direct prayer? How does an hour of prayer differ from an hour of worship?

During your prayer time, you should be communicating with God. Your entire inner spirit should be listening for what He has to say to you. Your whole focus needs to be on your relationship with the Lord and on your personal conversation.

Of course, the Bible plays a part. It is, after all, God's words to you. But active *study* of the Bible should be done outside of prayer. The same is true of other devotional material. Reading and studying either the Bible or other religious materials are necessary but can easily replace active prayer and become a substitute for actually talking to God.

Use Bible verses as springboards into the presence of God. Meditate on a text or phrase, and let the beauty of the text wash over you; experience its multifaceted meaning. Combined with prayer, this type of Bible reading brings a personal and relevant understanding to the words of God.

Bible texts that you use in prayer will often be drawn from Bible study you have done at other times. A compilation of Bible texts, divided up into sections pertinent to different situations like "Joy" or "Grief," will sometimes provide a passage specific to your present need. The Lord will often plant a particular text into your mind while you are praying, helping you to understand His will for you more fully.

The point here is not to exclude Bible study from prayer, but not to allow it to take central stage, squeezing out your time talking to God. You might get so caught up reading a passage of Scripture that your prayer time ends before you've even begun to approach God with your concerns of the day.

Music

A good friend of mine often uses music as part of her prayer time. You can use music as a mood setter by putting on soft, inspirational music without words. Or you can play a song, like a praise song, whose words are part of what you want to communicate with God. At other times, a song might convey a particular feeling you have at the moment as in times of extreme sadness or joy.

Creating music on the piano or an instrument, or singing it yourself, is another way to include music in prayer. Music is especially helpful to describe feelings of praise to God, something we have a hard time expressing. Other songs or choruses are invitations to God, such as "Into My Heart," "Just As I Am," "Alleluia," etc. As with Bible study, music can also take the place of prayer if you aren't careful. Make sure the music you choose adds to your actual prayer experience and is not a distraction away from prayer.

Nature

Using a place in nature as a prayer spot has already been mentioned in the previous chapter. But nature can also be used as part of prayer. Like the Bible, nature is God's way of talking *to* you directly. There are various ways you can make nature part of prayer.

Start or end your prayer by taking time to view nature. If you are lucky enough to have a beautiful view from your house or office, just sit back and let God talk to you. If your view isn't the best, pick something around you that still communicates from God. We bought a house with a "woods view" only to discover that seventy-five new homes were being built across the street. But even when they took down most of the trees and the acreage across from us was a mud pit, if I lay on my bed, I could see the tops of the distant trees out the window, silhouetted in their beauty against the sky.

Bring something into your prayer spot from nature that communicates from God. Nature is full of tiny, miraculous lessons about the love of God. Examine a leaf, a flower, a bug, or a rock. Proverbs says, "Go to the ant, you sluggard" (Proverbs 6:6), for a great spiritual lesson.

Sometimes it's nice to make nature the entire focus of your prayer by going for a walk or finding a great spot to pray in. And don't forget to pray those times you stumble into a splendid sunset or discover a jewel lake or watch with wonder as a squadron of geese heads home.

Following the ACTS format

Probably the simplest and easiest prayer format to follow is called the ACTS format. In use in Christian circles for a long time, ACTS stands for Adoration, Confession, Thanksgiving, and Supplication. This easy-to-remember acronym divides prayer into four main categories:

A—Adoration. Adoration is best translated "praise." I found this the hardest section of my prayer. It seemed foreign to my upbringing to actively praise God for just being God without tacking on the added dimension of thanksgiving.

The psalmist says, "I will extol the Lord at all times; his praise will always be on my lips" (Psalm 34:1). David was a master at praise; his psalms ring with adoration for God. If you are having trouble learning how to praise, just take a quick look through the Psalms, and you'll find plenty of material. Sometimes it is nice to start your prayer by reading a favorite psalm or reciting a portion you have memorized.

I often find the words to a praise chorus running through my mind as I begin my prayer. Playing praise music or singing songs of praise can help set the mood. Remember, if it doesn't come naturally, all you need is a little bit of practice.

Another helpful way to accustom yourself to praise is to think of a certain attribute of God each day. One day you might praise Him for being the Good Shepherd. Another day you might want to praise Him for being the Creator of the universe. And still another day, focus on His characteristics as a Father.

It is only fitting that you should begin your prayer to God with praise. It is too easy to come to God burdened by the problems of the day and start off, "Dear Jesus, please fix this or that." Starting your prayer with praise forces you to relax, slow down, and appreciate just whom you are approaching.

C—Confession. Although we may have a little more experience with confession than with adoration, most people haven't learned to move past "forgive my sins, and let's leave it at that." Maybe it would help to understand just why we are confessing. Is it to tell God what we've done wrong? Well, no, not if you believe He already knows everything. Is it to gain forgiveness of sins so if we die in the night we'll go to heaven? Yes, God requires Christians to ask forgiveness for their sins so that Jesus' blood can cleanse them.

If that's the only reason we have for confession, then a quick blanket "forgive my sins" is all we need. But I believe God wants us to use the time of confession not only to receive forgiveness, but also to receive understanding and enlightenment to help us grow and mature.

Imagine a member of your family who continually comes in the door, cuts through a corner of the dining room, and knocks a piece of china onto the floor. Every day this happens, and every day the person says, "Sorry about breaking the china," and walks away. Wouldn't somebody eventually say, "Why does this keep happening? What can we do to stop it?"

By taking time to think about the mistakes we've made during the day, we may actually realize what it is we are doing and then be in a position to do something to rectify the situation. Bill Hybels puts it this way: "I determined that in my prayers, I would deal with sin specifically. I would say, 'I told so-and-so there were nine hundred cars in the parking lot when really there were only six hundred. That was a lie, and therefore I am a liar. I plead for your forgiveness for being a liar.' "*

I realized that it was easy to glibly pray for forgiveness of sins while feeling inside as though I really hadn't sinned. When I actually thought about what I had done during the day, there were some startling revelations. I began to notice a pattern of being inwardly critical of other people. I would think, *My, that person really looks like a slob*, or, *I could have done that presentation better than he did*. I was especially bad when I was driving, making comments to myself about certain drivers' mental capabilities. I never realized I indulged in that habit until I took the time to examine it during prayer.

Good Christians often get caught in the little things—the slight exaggeration, the somewhat unethical business dealing. When you call sin by its right name—lying and stealing—it puts things into a whole new focus. During my confession times, the Lord convicted me about those gray areas, and I felt the necessity of rectifying some of them. It's embarrassing when you go into a store and say, "You accidently didn't charge me for this item, and I didn't say anything; but when I got home I felt bad and decided to bring it back." Store clerks look at you like you're nuts when you do that. It cures the gray habit in a hurry and keeps you from doing that type of silly gray thing again.

Once I was with a group who had gone to eat at a restaurant and parked in the mall's parking garage. The restaurant had a three-hour wait, so we decided to go somewhere else to eat but realized we would have to pay for parking. Usually parking was free if you had your ticket validated at the restaurant. Some of the group slipped up to the maitre d's desk in the crowded lobby and got their tickets validated anyway, even though we hadn't eaten there. I was tempted to do that. We could pull it off and, after all, we *had* tried to eat there. But it just wasn't worth squirming under the Lord's gaze during confession time and having to finally make things right with the restaurant in order to clear things up with God.

Another reason for spending time in confession is a long-term one. During your confession times, the Lord can convict you about habits or activities that you may be doing that are harmful to your relationship with Him. As you listen for His direction in your life, He will show you the next step to take. I find it's best to take that step as quickly as possible, whether or not you understand or even agree with it. If you don't, God will bring you back to the same point over and over again until you finally relinquish control. Until that happens, it is impossible to progress in your relationship, because everything builds one step at a time.

The time of confession can be painful, but it is also an important time of self-discovery. Here is where you see progress in your life; here is where you see the invigorating power of God, reaching into your innermost soul and leaving behind a shining heart. "If we confess our sins, he is faithful and just and will forgive us our sins and purify us from all unrighteousness" (1 John 1:9). Take time to listen. Let God dig and rake in your heart, clearing and pruning and creating a thing of beauty.

T—Thanksgiving. By the time you reach this section of your prayer, you have much to be thankful for. Already you have discovered the awesomeness of God and realized His careful management of your growth.

When you start listing the blessings God has given you, even the bleakest of lives will seem rich. I am continually amazed at how much we have to be thankful for, even during times when our family was going through extreme hardship. It's good to regularly make a list of blessings and things to be thankful for as a continual reminder of how much God cares.

S—Supplication. Notice that all the requests come at the end of your prayer. This format helps you to appreciate what part requests play in your relationship with God. First, you "seek after God," and then "all these things are added unto you."

Your list of requests to God is likely to get long and unwieldy. A little organization in this section goes far toward keeping your thoughts in order. The basis for that organization comes from the example of Jesus. Just prior to His arrest, He prays before going to the Garden of Gethsemane. That prayer is recorded in John 17. Jesus starts by praying for Himself and for His Father to be glorified. Next, He prays for the disciples and their protection from the world. Finally, He prays for all the believers down through the ages.

There is a wonderful symmetry to that organization. First, you start with yourself and any specific requests you have. Next, you move on to those closest to you: spouse, parents, children, siblings. Pray specifically for them and their needs. From there expand your circle to include people you have contact with regularly. These might be co-workers, school-mates, or other people you see regularly. Again, try to be specific in what you pray for. Your list might also include people you are aware of who need prayer for a particular problem right now: the child hit by a car, the friend battling with cancer, the relatives having marital problems.

In your circle, move on to your local church. Include members with particular needs. Pray for the leaders of your church and the pastor(s). Pray, too, for the Christian work in your area and the leaders of the worldwide mission. And don't forget to pray about political situations and world events.

Following a progression like this, in which you move from yourself to things farthest removed from yourself, helps you to cover everything and forget nothing. You will find there is a lot to pray about; many people are going through troublesome times and need a spiritual boost.

Review for a moment the entire ACTS format: time spent praising God for His greatness, a period of confession and listening for God's whispers of direction, jubilation and thanks-giving for His incredible mercies, and earnest supplication for yourself and those around you who need the care of the Lord. Now does it seem impossible to pray for ten minutes? Thirty minutes? An hour? If you really spend the time necessary to cover these sections well, you won't ever have a problem with finding something to say in prayer again.

As you put God first in your life and continue learning the art of a good conversation with Him, you will discover that your prayer time has become vibrant and alive! It's time well spent.

Prayer: Give me the creativity, Lord, to arrange my prayer time to facilitate optimum communication with You. Delight in me as I delight in You.

Practice: Pray using the ACTS format; Adoration, Confession, Thanksgiving, and Supplication.

---

* Bill Hybels, *Too Busy Not to Pray*, 54.

Chapter 5

The Wandering-Mind Syndrome

"Dear Lord,

I earnestly entreat You to forgive my sins today and to cleanse me. . . . Did I change the washing-machine setting from hot to cold when I put the coloreds in? I don't want that red T-shirt to bleed all over everything. . . . **Uh, Lord, uh, please be with me as I go about my activities today. . . .** I need to remember to pick up my dry cleaning; it's been three days. And the film is probably developed by now. And I really need to pick up some lettuce if we're going to have haystacks tonight. . . . **Oh, sorry. Help me to listen to Your voice today in everything I do. . . .** I need to buy a get-well card for Auntie Ivy, poor thing. I wonder how she's been doing since her hip operation. . . . **Yes, and be with Auntie Ivy and Jim, as he's struggling with finding a job, and Judy, whose husband is leaving her right now. . . .** I've got to remember to call the insurance people about that bill they sent. It just doesn't add up right. And while I'm at it, I should add roadside assistance onto the policy. . . . **Er, uhmmm, and so, Lord, please prepare us for Your kingdom, that we may be with You in the clouds of glory. . . .** They say it's not going to rain today, so I really need to water the garden before I head to work. If I hurry, I can do that and pick up the dry cleaning without being late. . . . **Thank You for Your loving care. Amen."**

Does that sound at all familiar? As a Christian, you've probably experienced the "wandering-mind syndrome" before. You start out worshiping the Lord and end up wondering about last night's football score.

Dealing with distractions requires the active participation of our will. Brother Lawrence says:

> Let it be *your* business to keep your mind in the presence of the Lord. If it sometimes wander and withdraw itself from Him, do not much disquiet yourself for that: trouble and disquiet serve rather to distract the mind than to recollect it; the will must bring it back in tranquillity. If you persevere in this manner, God will have pity on you.[1]

The written word

One of the best methods to keep your attention on your prayers is to write them down. There are many different ways to do this, so pick a method that works best for you.

Often called journaling, keeping a record of your prayers and your spiritual concerns is a wonderful way to chart your spiritual growth. A well-kept journal can be a never-ending source of material for talks or articles, Bible studies, and conversations. Also, prayer journals are great for reviewing God's past leading at times when you need to see the hand of God in your life.

Start by buying a notebook. You can use a simple essay book, a school notebook, or a blank hardback book with a decorative cover. Some people prefer using a three-ring binder so they can divide their notebook into sections and add or remove material.

Many people write in their journals every day. I found that I felt guilty if I skipped a day, and soon my journal became a chore. What worked better for me was to write when I felt like it or had something to say. This meant that my entries were much more heartfelt and true to my experience. You can either write just a summary of what you are praying about or write in detail about a specific request or problem. Some people write out their entire prayer. I found this a bit laborious to do all the time, but I found it very emotionally clarifying to write out a prayer if I was upset.

A journal is helpful for more than just writing prayers. Use it to jot down ideas that God puts in your mind, things you discover in your Bible reading, directions from God that come during your prayer time, or analogies or parables that help highlight spiritual concepts. It is this kind of journal that can become an incredible resource for you.

Becky Tirabassi has produced *My Partner Prayer Notebook,* which accompanies her book *Releasing God's Power.* This notebook contains sections such as Admit, Requests, Listening, and Thanks, among others. I used this system for a while—and it works nicely. The three-ring binder also worked well: I liked to be able to add or rearrange material.

A resource journal should include these five basic sections: Thanksgiving/Praise, Confession, Requests, Messages (from the Bible or other inspirational reading), and Listening (ideas and concepts God has given you). Make sure you date each entry so you can look back and see when things happened. Your time with God is precious; keep a record of what you learn.

Meditation

Along with talking *to* God, you need to allow time for Him to respond. Include time for meditation in your prayers. Instead of talking nonstop, leave quiet spaces in which He can respond. Psalm 46:10 says, "Be still and know that I am God." All our lives we are trained to be active, energetic, and productive. Now you must retrain yourself to just "be still" and let God come to you in His own time, to communicate to you what He wants you to hear. You will need to practice being still; it doesn't come naturally.

During times of meditation, it is especially easy to lose your concentration and be sidetracked by the day's activities and worries. If you have properly set up a prayer place and time, some of those distractions will already have been taken care of. But for the rest, here are some suggestions.

First, write down everything you have to do today or tomorrow on a list before you begin to pray. Once your agenda is on a list, your mind won't have to try to keep track of it anymore.

Offer the list to God while you seek Him in prayer.

During the writing of this chapter, I lost my wallet, something that ranks a nine on a stress scale of one to ten. I've been worrying about canceling credit cards, getting a new driver's license, and all those other phone calls and errands that have to be done to rectify the problem. But I knew I couldn't write in that frame of mind, so I asked God to take away my worries while I spent the time writing. Although the problem is not yet solved, I am free to pursue my time with Him, knowing He will take care of me no matter what happens to the wallet.

If a distracting thought pops into your head during prayer, try this focusing tip. Imagine a rushing stream flowing past your prayer place. When a distracting thought occurs, throw it in the stream, and let the current carry it away.

Listening to God can also come through reading His Word. After you have prayed, read a short biblical passage, looking for His answer. Often a text you have read many times before will suddenly jump to prominence in your reading, and you will see God's words for your life. In fact, praying without listening to God through His written words or through His impressions on your heart is really incomplete. Together, they form a whole conversation with God.

Meditation sometimes has disturbing connotations to the Christian, who may view it as part of the teachings of Eastern religions. But meditation as practiced by the Eastern mystics is actually a counterfeit of true meditation as originally instituted by God. The purpose of meditation is to clear your mind of all other thoughts so that it is open to guidance. As a Christian, the only reason you would clear your mind so that it is open to suggestion is within the context of prayerful seeking after God. Any other type of meditation would leave you open to suggestions you may not want to entertain. So don't be afraid to clear the rubble from your mind so that God can speak to you.

I like to think of this quiet time, listening for God's words to you and basking in His love, as "marinating" in Jesus. The more you know Him, the more you soak in His nearness; the more you know Him, the more every fiber, every cell of your body, is saturated with His presence.

Imagination

An active imagination can really help your experience with God. Imagine meeting with Jesus every morning in the place where you pray. See how impatient He is for you to join Him and start the conversation. Watch the expressions on His face as He listens to your troubles, rejoices with you in your triumphs, and sorrows with you over a setback. Jesus is truly involved in your prayer in this way. Make it real in your own mind.

Create a place where you can meet with Him for your communion. Maybe you feel closely attuned to God while in a beautiful spot in nature, such as beside a lake or waterfall or in a garden. Imagine being back in that spot, in its quietness and beauty, and carrying on a conversation with God there. The old hymn "In the Garden" expresses this idea:

> I come to the garden alone,
> While the dew is still on the roses;
> And the voice I hear,
> Falling on my ear,
> The Son of God discloses.
> And He walks with me, and He talks with me,
> And He tells me I am His own,
> And the joy we share as we tarry there,
> None other has ever known.

You can also imagine a place you would like to meet Jesus in the future—like on the streets of the New Jerusalem or beside the crystal sea. Actively using your imagination not only will help to make your experience more vivid, but also will help to cut down on mental distraction during your prayer time.

Prayer lists

Even following the ACTS format, it is still easy to forget somebody or something that you wanted to bring before God in prayer. Keeping a prayer list available can jog your memory and serve as a prayer record.

In your prayer notebook or on another piece of paper, write down your prayer requests as they occur. Date them, and leave space to write the answer to the request and the date the answer occurs. This prayer log will help you see when and how your prayers are answered.

When you reach the supplication portion of your prayer, you can look over your current prayer requests and add others that come to mind. Pray specifically for each request, or, as a variation, present the entire list to God.

Setting up a schedule

Once you have found prayer methods that are comfortable and productive, you can arrange your daily prayer time so you cover everything in an organized way. You will find a style and a schedule that works best for you, and as circumstances in your life change, you may have to rework your prayer schedule every so often.

Here are ways various people have structured their daily prayer schedule. These illustrations will give you ideas of how you can personalize your prayer time to fit your schedule and your needs:

Bill Hybels, senior pastor of the 11,000-member Willow Creek Church near Chicago, arranges his prayer time in the early morning. A corner of his office is his prayer place furnished with items that will help him draw closer to God. His commitment is to spend from half an hour to an hour every single morning in a secluded place with God.

When Bill begins his prayer time, his mental engine is racing at high RPMs, so his first activity is to slow down. First, he writes just one page, titled, "Yesterday" in a spiral notebook. By the time he is through detailing the activities of the previous day, he has begun to slow down and become receptive. Next, Bill writes out one page of prayer, following the ACTS format. When he finishes writing, he kneels in his prayer place and reads over his prayer, adding and embellishing his comments. Says Hybels:

When I have done that, my spirit is quiet and receptive. That is when I write an L for *listen* on a piece of paper and circle it. Then I sit quietly and simply say, "Now, Lord, I invite you to speak to me by your Holy Spirit."

The moments with God that follow are the ones that really matter. This is where authentic Christianity comes from.[2]

Author and speaker Becky Tirabassi's prayer regimen evolved into *My Partner Prayer Notebook*, which has sold thousands of copies.

Becky made a contract to pray for a minimum of one hour every day, a promise she has not broken in over six years. Her prayer place is her kitchen table, where she prepares herself with pen and paper. This is how she divides her hour:

Her notebook has two sections—her part and God's part. In her part the acronym PART stands for Praise, Admit, Requests, and Thanksgiving—the basic components of the ACTS format. During each hour, Becky journals her thoughts in each section. In the Praise section, she finds several praise psalms that she rewrites as her own personal praise prayers as a preparation for her time with God.

God's part of the notebook is labeled LMNOP. *L* is for Listening to God. *M* is a place to jot down ideas from sermons or talks. *N*, *O*, and *P* are sections to write pertinent verses from the New Testament, Old Testament, and Proverbs. The final section is labeled "To Do"—a place to list all those things you need to do that pop into your mind during your prayer time.

Becky says of her system:

My hour with God became an organized appointment. I was daily growing to understand the spiritual discipline of prayer, its incredible importance in the life of a believer, more of God's character, the concept of faith, and the practicality of time spent in written conversation with God.[3]

Many people have been blessed by the spiritual journey of

author Sue Monk Kidd, recorded in her book *God's Joyful Surprise*. She explains how she fashions her times of intense, meditative prayer. First, she found a time and place to meet with God. In her case it was after her husband and children had left for the day. Her special place was a green leather chair at her desk with a small brass cross in front of her.

Sue found, when she began to pray meditatively, that she was too tense, and there was too much inner noise to really focus on God. So her first task was to relax the body. She did this through a series of exercises, contracting and relaxing all the muscles of her body, working from the toes up. The next task was to relax the mind. Sue imagined Christ calming a storm on the Sea of Galilee in her own mind until there was only the lap, lap, lapping of the quiet waves, and then silence.

Another device she used was the idea of a "circle of quiet."

> I suddenly imagined Christ drawing a circle around me. I sat in the middle of the circle, which was shining like a ring of light. Inside there was a hush, a deep still calmness. A Presence. Christ assured me nothing could penetrate the circle from the outside, but that I could send all my concerns, fears, frustrations and thoughts outside the circle. One by one I mentioned the things weighing on my mind, imagining them moving outside the circle.[4]

At that point Sue was able to fully concentrate on what God had to say to her.

In her "prayer of presence," she simply tried to be there for God, in His presence, listening for His voice. That kind of intense concentration, waiting in God's presence, has to be practiced, maybe for five minutes a day at first, then ten, fifteen, and even twenty.

I have found the ACTS format the most helpful in organizing my prayer time. During my prayer times with God, I find I remember everything I need to pray about. I can shorten or lengthen the prayer according to my available time and amount of subject material.

Journaling has become the most tangibly rewarding of my prayer disciplines. Having such a clear record of what I am feeling and what God is saying is like keeping a photo album of a special trip. It's wonderful to look through it with fond memories, and it also provides valuable resource material.

I found that my list of people to pray for grew cumbersome in the ACTS format, so I divided it up into two parts. The permanent people and requests on my list I prayed for in the mornings. The temporary requests, along with the normal progression I used during the Supplication section of ACTS, I prayed for in the evening, when I had my longer time with God.

Another thing I practice is praying for protection and guidance in the morning and forgiveness in the evening. I feel it's important to start my day by first turning over my life, my activities, and my emotions to God to guide as He sees fit. I also invite the Holy Spirit into my life to be my companion during the day.

In the evening I make sure I spend time during the confession portion of ACTS asking forgiveness for sins of the day and asking God to complete the work He has started in me by rooting out anything ugly inside.

This way of beginning and ending the day puts a wonderful spiritual "sandwich" on all my thoughts and activities, wraps up the entire day, and turns it over to God.

Prayer: Lord, give me focus in my prayers. Help me to minimize the distractions and to concentrate entirely on You.

Practice: Choose one of the following.
•Draw a picture of the ideal place in which you would like to meet Jesus to talk.
•Write out a prayer.

---

1. Brother Lawrence, *The Practice of the Presence of God*, 50, 51.
2. Bill Hybels, *Too Busy Not to Pray*, 119.
3. Becky Tirabassi, *Releasing God's Power*, 70.
4. Sue Monk Kidd, *God's Joyful Surprise: Finding Yourself Loved* (San Francisco: Harper & Row, 1987), 196, 197.

Chapter 6

Where Two or Three Are Gathered

The news was devastating. James, the brother of John, one of the most devout followers of Jesus, had been put to death. The message spread like wildfire through the new Christian community. The remaining disciples grieved for him and for the future of their church.

But while they were still mourning for James, a second shock wave followed the first. Simon Peter, the backbone of the struggling church, had just been arrested and was destined to follow James's sad fate.

The believers met together to comfort one another and to discuss what could be done. But mostly they met to pray together, to lift Peter up before God and place his life in God's hands. They asked for God's protection over their earnest little band, for the death of Peter could be a serious blow to the budding church. They prayed for faith, no matter what happened. They prayed in God's will. They prayed and wept into the morning hours, supporting one another's faith with verses of Scripture and the remembered words of Jesus.

Can you see them sitting in a circle around a flickering candle, their faces wet with tears but the corners of their mouths lifting in tremulous smiles as one recalled a treasured conversation with Jesus, another recalled the joy on a friend's face as he was suddenly infused with a surging power that drove him to walk again for the first time in years, and still another recalled a promised blessing for those who faced trials?

Late one night, as they were gathered for prayer, there came a knock on the door. With apprehension, they watched the servant girl hurry to the door. Only soldiers came calling in the middle of the night. But to their astonishment and joy, Peter walked into the room with an incredible story to tell of his rescue from prison by an angel of God, sent in response to the earnest prayers of that little band of believers.

Prayer is exponential. Put one prayer together with another, and you have not two, but four. Put four together, and you have, not eight, but sixteen. The power that is realized when a group of people come together to approach the throne of God in prayer is overwhelming. One flickering flame may sputter and waver; its faith may struggle to keep the flame alive. But put it together with another flame and another and another, and soon you'll have a whole forest fire.

When you are struggling to walk the narrow path by yourself, it can be cold and dark and awfully lonely. But buoyed by the faith and support of a group of believers, you'll find that the road looks much less desolate. I'm sure that's part of the reason Jesus called the Twelve to follow Him. Although He had to spend long hours teaching them the truth about the kingdom He was offering, by the end of their three years together, they were beginning to understand and to support Jesus in His ministry.

When Jesus agonized in the Garden of Gethsemane, He did not pray alone. Rather, He brought His three closest disciples to participate with Him in this darkest of nights, when earth's ultimate destiny would be decided.

Surely as God, Jesus would not need anyone to pray with Him. But Jesus was also human, and His human nature cried out for human touch, another heart to share the burden, another soul to beseech God on His behalf, another friend to watch and pray with Him.

Unfortunately, the devil realized the importance of this prayerful support to Jesus and brought all his seducing powers to bear on the disciples to do the most natural thing—sleep. The Lord endured alone that awful night.

We, however, are not called to carry the burdens of the world, or even of our own family, on our own slender shoulders. God has provided for prayerful spiritual bonding and support between people who share His name. Jesus tells us in Matthew 18:19, 20:

> Again, I tell you that if two of you on earth agree about anything you ask for, it will be done for you by my Father in heaven. For where two or three come together in my name, there am I with them.

M. Scott Peck describes the process that a group working together goes through to eventually achieve what he calls "community," a group of individuals who have learned how to communicate honestly with each other, whose relationships go deeper than their masks of composure, and who are committed to experiencing each other's emotions. Once a group has achieved community, it is characterized by a spirit of peace.

> The spirit of community is not envisioned as a purely human spirit or one created solely by the group. It is assumed to be external to and independent of the group. It therefore is thought of as descending upon the group, just as the Holy Spirit is said to have descended upon Jesus at his baptism in the form of a dove. . . . Thus for those of Christian orientation the work of community building is seen as preparation for the descent of the Holy Spirit. The spirit of community is a manifestation of the Holy Spirit.[*]

By praying together regularly, the early believers became a community receptive to the Holy Spirit at Pentecost. The same principles apply today; only you seldom find a group of believers gathered together in earnest prayer.

Find added blessings through prayer partners
Having a prayer partner is much different from having a close friend. When two people meet regularly to pray, they are bonded in a unique way. If you are married and pray regularly

with your spouse, you understand how prayer can bring an added closeness.

When I learned about the added dimension that a prayer partner can bring, I began praying that the Lord would lead me to someone with whom I could pray. A couple of months later I was at a convention, where I got to know better an acquaintance of mine. As we talked, I realized that here was someone who shared my spiritual interests. Not only that, but she was within driving distance of where I lived in the country—no easy feat!

Eventually I got up my courage to ask if she might be interested in being my prayer partner—and discovered that she was thinking of asking me! It was a real sign that God was blessing my increasing interest in the subject of prayer.

Unless your prayer partner is your spouse, a prayer partner should be of the same sex, since shared prayer can bring an emotional intimacy. Sometimes a good friendship will grow out of a prayer friendship as well; sometimes prayer partners will never meet socially at all. But whatever the relationship, prayer partners understand the added blessing of praying with another person.

Several things happen when you pray with a partner:

Prayer partners learn accountability. My husband likes to boast of a time in his life during which he exercised regularly every morning at a local gym and really expanded his fitness level. He faithfully got up at 5:30 a.m. to exercise before his classes began. But then, he will be quick to admit that a friend of his, who also went to the gym every morning, was even more regular. Knowing that the friend would be waiting at the club was what got my husband to drag his body out of bed so early, even when he didn't feel like it.

If it works for exercise, it surely ought to work for prayer. Having a regularly scheduled appointment for prayer and having someone waiting for you can really help to keep you going. You have an obligation to be there for the other person, and once you're there, the power of prayer will recapture you. If you find that you become easily discouraged in your spiritual life, that your prayers don't seem to be going anywhere, praying regularly with a partner can help to rejuvenate your spiritual batteries and give you added incentive to continue.

Not only are you accountable to a partner to keep praying regularly, but you are also accountable to him or her in your spiritual life. If you are honest with each other, your partner will know when you are having a tough spiritual battle and can pray you through it. It's good to have someone you can confess to when your spiritual life isn't up to par or when you're having some problems. "Therefore confess your sins to each other and pray for each other so that you may be healed. The prayer of a righteous man is powerful and effective" (James 5:16).

Praying together broadens your spiritual mind. Two heads are better than one, it has been said, especially when they are bowed in prayer. Sometimes if you are confused as to how God is leading you, a partner may have a clearer picture of what you're experiencing. An insightful word at the right moment can open the door to a new concept.

I'll always be grateful to my prayer partner for pointing me to the basics. After we had talked for a while about our personal troubles, she would say, "Now, let's pray." I would sometimes try to keep talking about the problem, but she would insist, "You'll feel better after you have prayed." She was right. Instead of talking around and around the problem, I needed to directly approach God with it. The solution always seemed much clearer when we were through praying.

Prayer partners help others. The first person you help is your partner, because just as she helps you keep focused with God, you help her too. A prayer partner should have a place on your permanent prayer list; her spiritual journey is now your concern, and you should continually keep her before God. My prayer partner began to fall away after a while. I still don't know what happened. But I think she was going through some tough things in her life that she was unwilling to share even with me. Although I was hurt, I continued to pray for her for a long time, and I often wondered if God had brought us together so that I would be praying for her during a difficult time in her life.

God says that when two of you agree here on earth, heaven moves to answer the prayer. As you pray for yourselves and each other, you will soon expand your prayers to include other people who need God's power in their lives. It is a relief to share the burden of a wayward child, an unbelieving husband, a friend with a serious illness, with someone else.

How do you find a special person like this? There are no easy answers. You may know of someone right away who could fill that spot in your life. But I think your best course of action is to place an ad with the heavenly personals: Wanted—one spiritual person to pray with. If you are interested in a prayer partner, make it a sincere and consistent prayer request that God will bring you the right person. Don't give up if someone doesn't knock on your door the next morning. God will take care of you in His time.

I had been praying awhile for another person or group to pray with. It didn't happen right away, and I wasn't sure why God hadn't chosen to answer that prayer yet. But I knew that He would bring the blessing in His own time. Remarkably, God led me to a new prayer partner during the writing of this section!

It is up to you and your partner to decide on your own schedule and location. Meeting once a week or once every two weeks probably is the easiest. My partner and I alternated between our two homes; you might find another place to meet such as a church or a park or even at your place of business. Wherever you meet, make sure it is a place where you can indulge in long periods of prayer without feeling uncomfortable.

You and your partner need to allow time to talk about what's going on in your lives and in the lives of those for whom you're praying. Then both of you should pray—you both need the benefit of talking to God, as well as being prayed for. Because the most important time for prayer partners is when their hearts are joined in prayer, approaching the throne of grace together, it is vital to allow yourselves enough time so that neither of you feels rushed and you both can cover all your concerns.

Become part of a prayer group

If there is a group at your church or school that is already meeting or is interested in prayer, form a prayer group. Prayer groups can take many forms and can schedule their meetings in many different ways, but they all have one common function: to pray. Like prayer partners, prayer groups have accountability in prayer and to each other.

A weekly or biweekly schedule works best. Even a monthly meeting can be inspiring if you meet for a longer period of time. The group can range from three to three hundred, but a small group of from six to twelve is ideal because it gives everyone a chance to pray without feeling terribly rushed. You also become better acquainted in a smaller group.

Prayer groups can take a number of forms:

Prayer meeting. You probably are familiar with the prayer-meeting format, which usually meets on Wednesday evenings at the church. Prayer meetings differ from typical prayer groups in that their size is not limited and often fluctuates widely with each meeting.

Many prayer meetings are usually conducted like a regular religious service with everyone sitting in rows and most of the communication coming from the front. To make the meeting more personal, try having everyone sit comfortably in a circle— or if you have a small group, meet at someone's house. Encourage everyone's participation in the group so no one person does most of the talking. Make prayer the focus of the meeting and not just the conclusion.

Fellowship prayer group. A fellowship prayer group is usually smaller and more casual than a prayer meeting. Usually meeting in people's homes, a fellowship prayer group may start with snacks or a meal and then move on to the prayer time. Women's and men's prayer breakfasts or brunches follow this format.

I belonged to a small group like this for a while, and it was always a highlight of the week. We spent some time in fellowship and sharing before we got into our subject of study. Sometimes a book of the Bible was our topic; other times someone would suggest a devotional or religious book that we would study during the week and discuss at the meeting.

Prayer was always the focal point, and we made sure to keep a record of our prayer requests.

There are many ways to structure a group like this. Someone may act as the leader of the group and do most of the teaching. Or, as in our case, group members take turns leading the discussion each week. We moved from home to home for our meetings as people volunteered, but because a couple members had children, we met more often at their homes so they could participate.

Although evening seems to be the preferable time, early-morning prayer groups do meet, and there may even be some that could meet during lunch. Some young mothers' groups will meet in the mornings after school starts. The mothers' group at our church meets every Wednesday morning, and they all chip in to pay for a baby sitter during that time.

You can decide together what you will study or whether you want to make prayer your entire focus. Try to preserve the time you have for prayer, because it is easy to "run out of time" and cut the prayer time short. It may be helpful to pray first and study later.

Intercessory prayer group. Although intercessory prayer will be part of any prayer group, an intercessory prayer group meets solely for the purpose of praying for the needs of others. They spend their prayer time bringing various people and situations before God.

Our church has an intercessory prayer group that meets once a month at 9:00 a.m. before Sabbath School begins. Its purpose is to pray specifically for our church, the members' requests, and for the church services.

Form a telephone or chain prayer group

It's nice to know in a time of crisis or discouragement that there is someone available to pray for you. Some churches have a telephone committee whose purpose is to get messages to the members. Why not form a telephone prayer chain, whose purpose is to pray for the members?

After we started a telephone prayer chain at our church, I

was surprised how much it was used. People even called long distance to have their requests put on the chain. We publish the number every week in our church bulletin, so it is available to everyone.

The telephone prayer chain works very simply. You start with a group of people who are near a phone during the day and can be interrupted for prayer when necessary. One person is the "chairperson," or the start of the chain. This person is responsible to keep a log of all the calls that come to the chain. It is his or her phone number that is listed in the bulletin. The rest of the members are assigned to call the next person on the chain. When a request comes in, the leader logs it in a journal, prays for the request, and then calls the next person on the chain. Each member prays for the request before calling the next chain member.

In just a few minutes, you have a whole group of people praying for a person in need. It is a very comforting feeling to know God's people can respond so quickly.

It is God's plan that His church will be filled with members who really care about each other, who will take the time to pray for one another and to be there to lend a listening ear or a strong arm. If you are serious about growing stronger in your prayer relationship with God, don't pass up the opportunity to bolster your prayer time with the help of other Christian believers.

Prayer: God, please bring me into contact with a prayer partner (or partners) with whom I can experience the fellowship of communal prayer.

Practice: Make a point of finding someone with whom to pray this week.

---

* M. Scott Peck, *The Different Drum: Community-Making and Peace* (New York: Simon & Schuster, Inc., 1987), 75.

Chapter 7

Incredible Intercession

"Has your husband ever considered going into the ministry?" I asked my friend.

She smiled and answered, "It's funny you should ask that. Our church pastor was encouraging him just the other day to become a minister."

Little did she know what an answer to prayer her comment was for me.

It had started three years earlier, when I was part of an intercessory prayer group. Each of us were to pick three names that we wanted to pray for especially. I had two, but I couldn't decide on a third, so I asked God to impress me about whom else I should pray. The answer I received seemed odd. I knew very little about this person, but from what I had seen, although he didn't seem particularly spiritual, he also didn't seem as if he needed converting.

When the impression wouldn't go away, I finally asked the Lord what I should pray for in regard to this individual. The impression came that I should pray about his going into the ministry. Well, that seemed even more out of character for him, especially since he had expressed an interest in medicine. But since I didn't feel impressed to pray for anyone else, I added him to the list.

For almost three years, I prayed for him. I still knew nothing at all about his spiritual condition, and he certainly hadn't gone into the ministry.

Eventually, we visited him and his wife for the weekend. I was impressed with how, as young adults, they were still

65

interested in church and spiritual things. Then his wife began telling me how her husband had experienced a time of dramatic spiritual growth the previous few years. How he had become very spiritual and had surprised even her. That was when I asked about his going into the ministry and received her surprising reply. Yes, he had thought about the ministry but hadn't decided yet what area he was called to serve in.

The neat thing about this answer to intercessory prayer was that it was so blind. Often when you pray for someone, the need is obvious; you can see that the person is an alcoholic or he isn't attending church or he is struggling with diabetes. But, in this case, the Lord impressed me to pray for someone I hardly knew, someone who lived a thousand miles away, and without knowing why the individual was in need of prayer.

This situation showed me that God values our prayers for one another, that He puts a high priority on intercessory prayer in our spiritual lives, and that He makes a point to direct us to pray for people in need.

Why should we pray for others? Because it is an express command of our Lord Jesus Christ.

> I urge . . . that requests, prayers, intercession and thanksgiving be made for everyone—for kings and all those in authority. . . . This is good, and pleases God our Savior, who wants all men to be saved and to come to a knowledge of the truth (1 Timothy 2:1-3).

In the first chapter, I mentioned 1 Samuel 12:23. Not only did the passage say that lack of prayer is a sin, but the text says it is a sin to fail to "pray for *you*" (emphasis added).

What exactly does it mean to intercede for someone? Jesus is our intercessor before God: "Christ Jesus . . . is at the right hand of God and is also interceding for us" (Romans 8:34). In His role of intercessor, He steps into our place and does for us what we cannot or will not do for ourselves. When you intercede for someone, you are coming to God in his or her place, on his behalf.

Intercessory prayer is much more than the simple childhood prayer of "Bless Mommy and Daddy and the missionaries and colporteurs across the seas." As we grow in our prayer life, Jesus leads us to understand more fully the responsibility of praying for others.

In Matthew 5:44, Jesus urges His followers to "pray for those who persecute you." Why would you pray for someone who was actively persecuting you? These people certainly aren't doing any praying for themselves. They definitely need someone to bring their case before God.

The incredible act of Jesus' forgiving those who were crucifying Him was brought home to me by my wallet being stolen. Somewhere between chapters 5 and 6 I found out that, yes, my wallet had indeed been stolen; a custodian in an apartment complex had found my checkbook in the trash, along with someone else's credit cards.

So, I went down to the apartment complex and started my own hunt through the trash, looking for other missing items. What I found confirmed my suspicions as to who had taken my wallet. In the dumpster I found a photocopied page of information about our church that I had given someone who had dropped by the church two days before.

I had been extremely nice to this man, going out of my way to collect material for him and photocopying some pages of information for him to take with him. But it was that day my wallet was missing from my car.

When I pulled the photocopied page out of the dumpster, my blood ran cold for a moment. I was furious with him, and I wished I hadn't treated him so well. *I wonder what I would have said to him had I known he would steal from me*, I thought to myself. But then it hit me: in a spirit of true love, Christ—bleeding, tortured, and dying in agony—had interceded on behalf of His killers before God, asking that they be forgiven.

The petty crime that victimized me was insignificant compared to what Christ suffered—and He even knew in advance what would happen to Him. Could I actually love someone who would brazenly steal from me? Could I pray for him? Ask God to forgive him? When you suddenly understand the implications of the true Christian life, your complacency is shattered. This is what we are called to do as Christians. This is the true concept of intercession.

I see our interceding on behalf of someone else as giving the Holy Spirit permission to work in their lives.

> God never violates the free will of anyone, but when we pray for someone else, it permits Him to work in their lives with a special power. He unshackles the individual from the chains of sin so that he can use his freedom of choice to choose good.[1]

None of us are saved through our own good works; we are led to God by the gentle beckoning of the Spirit. By praying for someone, you give him or her a chance to be drawn in by God's irresistible love.

Principles of intercessory prayer

Start with yourself. Before you can intercede for someone else, you must make sure your own relationship with God is operating smoothly. Open your heart to be cleansed by God; let your motives be pure. God warns clearly that there are conditions for answering our prayers: "Your iniquities have separated you from your God; your sins have hidden his face from you, so that he will not hear" (Isaiah 59:2).

Pray in the mind of God. Without an intimate knowledge of God and His will, we don't know for what we should pray. Pray that God will show you *whom* to pray for and *what* to pray for in their lives. Many people have struggles that no one else is aware of, but God will show you who needs your prayers if you look for His guidance. During your prayer time, God will prepare you to accept the work that He has for you.

Pray for the Holy Spirit to be heard. Most people's lives are so filled with noisy static that it is almost impossible for them to hear the whisper of the Spirit. Pray specifically that they will hear that still, small voice, that circumstances in their lives will quieten enough for them to be aware of who is calling.

Remember, though, that everyone is given the power of choice. God does not force people to serve Him. If your prayers for someone to come to God are not answered, don't despair. It often takes a long time for someone to acquiesce to the Spirit's call. But remember, too, that neither you nor God can force someone to respond.

It is by the power of the Holy Spirit that our consciences are troubled and we begin to open up our lives to God. If you pray for the Holy Spirit to work with someone, you can be assured that he or she will begin to experience His power in their lives. Someone I know once commented that a friend I was praying for regularly seemed restless and unhappy in his life of sin. "I think the Holy Spirit is working with him," she commented. And truly, He was.

Pray for whatever it takes. This is a hard concept. Sometimes when we begin to pray for people, it seems their lives fall apart. Is God doing this? we ask.

> When once you see a soul in sight of the claims of Jesus Christ, . . . instead of putting out a hand to prevent the throes, pray that they grow ten times stronger until there is no power on earth or in hell that can hold that soul away from Jesus Christ.[2]

Someone for whom I have been praying for an extended period of time is presently going through an extremely trying time as his wife battles cancer. But for all the horror they are going through, I can see how much closer they have come to God as a result of their trials.

When you pray that God will do whatever it takes in a life, rejoice when you see evidence that His voice is being heard. But it doesn't mean that everything will now be perfect. There is still a lot of work ahead to clear out the old life and bring in the new. "You may often see Jesus Christ wreck a life before He saves it."[3]

Don't rush through your prayers. True communion with God

is not hurried. If you are sincerely burdened with the troubles of others, you won't treat your prayers for them liked a rushed "to do" list. Spend time in true intercession, praying for them and reading Scripture promises that apply to their situation. The practice of setting aside a specific length of time for prayer each day helps immeasurably in keeping you from feeling rushed during your prayers.

Be consistent in your prayers. A great biblical example of how God wants us to pray consistently is the story of Moses and the Amalekites. As the Israelites and the Amalekites were engaged in battle, Moses stood on a hilltop in prayer and supplication to God.

The Israelites were doing fine, so Moses stopped praying and started watching the battle. To his horror, the tide started to swing against the Israelites. Quickly he resumed his prayer position, and the Israelites soon gained the upper hand. After this had happened a few times, Moses finally caught on. But his arms were getting tired, so he sat on a rock, and Aaron and Hur held up his arms as he continued to entreat the Lord for victory (see Exodus 17:8-16).

The Lord wants us to be consistent in our prayers, to daily bring our requests before Him. Praying for people once a week, or whenever you remember, does not show your intense concern for their needs. If you have decided to take on people as your prayer responsibility, then their victory is "in your hands." Make sure you keep your arms raised to God in support of your prayer requests.

Along with consistency comes patience. Prayed-for changes in people's lives may not become obvious until after months or even years of praying. In this world that expects instant gratification, waiting patiently will take practice. But developing patience can benefit you as well, as the Lord develops your faith in His workings.

Pray for specific changes in a person's life. Certainly God will hear you if you pray for Him to "bless" someone, but why not pray for something specific? If someone is in need of spiritual help for a troubled marriage, pray especially that God will give both parties a spirit of peace and reconciliation. If someone needs help in overcoming an addiction, pray specifically that God will take away his desire for that substance.

Praying specifically not only helps to target your prayers where they are most needed, but also helps you to see more clearly when God answers your prayers. If you're not sure exactly what to pray for, ask God to help you.

Pray for the power of Satan to be broken in their lives. People who are not following God have given their power of choice over to Satan. He clouds their minds and makes it seem confusing for them to find God. Your intercession for them can restore to them clear thinking and spiritual understanding of the state of their lives. At that point they will be able to make choices for God. I like to imagine my prayers as being a flag of Jesus planted in their lives as claim to the territory.

When you pray, ask that the power of evil will be kept at bay so that they can feel the Spirit's influence. Don't be afraid to pray that God will forgive their sins. When Jesus was healing here on earth, He demonstrated that physical and mental healing logically followed spiritual healing. It was after He forgave the paralytic's sins that He raised him up to physical strength. By praying that God will forgive others' sins, you are asking Him to remove the burden of guilt and pain that they have been carrying. That forgiveness will leave them free to turn their thoughts toward spiritual things and receive the help they need.

Here are some practical ways to pray regularly for others:

Prayer lists. Keep a list of names that you want to pray for regularly. You can organize your list in several different ways. You might set up a page in your prayer journal for personal requests, a page for people you pray for regularly, and a page for temporary requests. Or, use a separate notebook as your prayer-request notebook.

I keep two prayer lists. One has items that are of a temporary nature: someone is ill; a friend needs prayer for a job interview; my husband needs protection for a journey. The other list has items that are more permanent: resolution for a marriage in conflict, a relative who needs to be won to Christ, prayer for someone with a long-term illness. The requests from this second list don't get forgotten by being covered up by a lot of temporary requests.

Make sure you keep a record of the answers you receive. Don't throw any prayer lists away, even short-term lists. It's exciting to look back and see what God has been doing.

A prayer group might like to set up a permanent prayer-request book. In this book keep a record of all the requests made by the members. Make sure you have a column for answered prayer and the date. The book can be left at the site where the group meets, or one member can be in charge of it.

We set up a prayer-request book in the lobby of our church. This book contains a space for the date, request, answer, and date answered. There is also a column for the name of the person making the request—but that is marked optional. That leaves people free to make requests without identifying themselves to the entire church.

I was surprised how much that book was used. The requests have been mentioned in the pastoral prayer and are used by members of the intercessory prayer group. Anyone who looks through the book can pray for the requests. It is encouraging to see the requests and answers that have been recorded there.

Prayer contracts. This fascinating application of intercessory prayer uses the idea of Matthew 18:20: "Where two or three come together in my name, there am I with them."

This idea works best in a very small group; three people is ideal. Each member chooses a certain number of names—again, three is ideal—that they want to pray especially for. These are people for whom you want to see a definite, specific, and dramatic change in their lives. The group makes up a master list of all the individuals and writes by each name what the specific prayer request is. Then each member covenants with the others to pray for *all* the names every single day. In a prayer group of three people, each with three requests, each individual would be praying every day for nine requests.

It is exciting to use this magnified prayer power. And it is comforting to know that there are others praying for your requests and sharing your burdens, as well. The prayer group can meet as often as they like to update each other on the progress made. When you hear your prayer partners telling about the amazing changes they see taking place in the people you are praying for, that is when you realize the magnitude and strength of prayer.

Intercessory prayer groups. Moses interceded on behalf of the Israelites in their battle against the Amalekites. But eventually Moses got tired, even though the battle was not over. It was then that Moses' friends, Aaron and Hur, stepped in to support him in the spiritual fight. Joining together with a group of individuals who are all earnestly praying and interceding on behalf of others gives energy and spiritual strength when fatigue and discouragement threaten to overwhelm.

An intercessory prayer group can "hold up each others' arms" in prayer, to be an unwavering force in the campaign against evil. An intercessory prayer group should remain small, preferably less than twelve, in order to retain a feeling of intimacy and bonding among the members as they work together. They should meet consistently and should devote the majority of the meeting to prayer.

The prayer requests can come from a number of places. First, the group members will have their own personal concerns—family and friends they want to pray for. Second, the group can pray for requests that come from their local church or school. These can be collected by means of a prayer-request book, a prayer-request box, or from prayer requests given verbally in church or school. Third, the group may decide on a particular ministry for which they want to pray.

A good example of this is the group Moms-in-Touch, a national organization with local chapters. The specific purpose of this intercessory group is for mothers of school-age children to pray together for their school, their teachers, and their children, and members are supplied with guidelines to follow when they join a chapter.

Other specific prayer ministries might be to pray for your church family as a whole; for the Holy Spirit to be poured out on your church; or for a particular project your church is attempting, such as expanding or starting a ministry for divorcees or beginning an evangelistic outreach. Or your intercessory prayer group can pray outside the scope of your local area and focus on foreign missions or even politics.

Special times of prayer. Occasionally, special circumstances require special times of intercessory prayer. The story of Peter in prison is a good example. Peter needed some major prayer power right then, and his friends got together to help.

•Pray for someone in crisis. Jesus often prayed all night when He was in need of His Father's help. Very few of us pray more than a couple of minutes about someone who is in crisis. When a person close to you is going through a major crisis situation, he or she may need CPR prayer. If you are not in a position to talk to her or help her in any way, prayer, then, is your only tool.

If you really care that someone you love is suffering in ICU or is about to destroy a relationship or is in danger of becoming addicted to drugs or alcohol, then take the phone off the hook, turn off the TV, go somewhere quiet, and really *pray*. Take half an hour or an hour or however long you can, and make that person your priority. Focus all your concentration on him; let your entire prayer be centered on his need. Imagine the Spirit encircling, protecting, and comforting him and gently shepherding him in the right direction. Pray for the enveloping arms of the Father, pray that his sins will be forgiven, that his mind will be at peace, that he will turn to the One who gives all strength. Certainly, you can spare half an hour in prayer for the one you love. Remember, Samuel says, "Far be it from me that I should sin against the Lord by failing to pray for you" (1 Samuel 12:23).

Sometimes the person in crisis may be you. Just as Jesus agonized in the Garden of Gethsemane, so you may need to come to the Lord in special prayer. Follow Jesus' example and bring praying friends with you.

•Pray for a temporary need. A small intercessory prayer group may be set up to pray for a certain period of time. They might pray regularly prior to the start of a series of meetings or before a major outreach program. One example is a church group that prayed for a month prior to a big weekend prayer seminar. They felt they could not go unprepared, "cold turkey," into such an important event.

•Pray in times of emergency. A large intercessory prayer group may form spontaneously when a sudden tragedy strikes a school or church. Often, classmates of someone who has been struck suddenly with leukemia or injured in some way will come together for an intensive period of CPR prayer.

A church or school might also come together as a large group to pray for the Holy Spirit to fill their congregation or for guidance in future plans. These intercessory groups are all temporary, occur in response to a need, and are specific in their content.

In your prayer journey, make sure you include time for intercession. Although many people don't fully understand the implications of praying intercessorily, be assured of this: God wants you to pray for others. In His prayers, Jesus gives us many examples in which He intercedes for those around Him. Jesus finishes His beautiful prayer in John 17 by praying for those in this world who do not know Him.

It is easy to become self-centered in prayer, to concentrate only on what prayer is doing for us. But a lot of people can use a prayer boost; a little extra strength to get through a rough time; a clear view of Christ, who stands beckoning. Be an intercessor for them.

Prayer: As I encounter people throughout my day, give me a burden to pray for them, Lord, to actively intercede on their behalf so that they may be drawn to You.

Practice: Start an intercessory prayer list. In a journal or note-book make a list of several people for whom you would like to pray on a regular basis. List the specific changes you would like to see in their lives and date your entry. Leave space for comments and answers.

---

1. Roger Morneau, *Incredible Answers to Prayer* (Hagerstown, Md.: Review and Herald, 1990), 12.
2. Oswald Chambers, *My Utmost for His Highest*, 60.
3. Ibid.

Chapter 8

The Door Will Be Opened

Answers to prayer are the least important part of your prayer life!

Those of you who skipped straight to this chapter to find out how to get an answer to prayer, go back right now and start from the beginning!

Sneaky, aren't they? But, seriously, if your only interest in prayer is wanting to learn how to get answered prayer, then you're starting at the wrong end of the equation. (That's the reason this chapter isn't at the beginning of the book.) We have so much to learn about prayer itself before we can truly understand the relevance of answered prayer. Too many of us would have to admit to being more interested in God's blessings than in God Himself.

To most people, the fact that God has never done anything miraculous or startling in answer to their prayers means that, at the very least, He doesn't care and possibly that He doesn't even exist. As you may have already found out, answers to prayer are illusory things. So many different formulas guaranteeing answers to prayer are proposed that you get the impression that if you cross your fingers under a full moon while reciting certain Bible verses in the correct order, you will be the lucky jackpot winner—sort of a cosmic abracadabra.

I've always been puzzled by Matthew 7:7, 8:

Ask and it will be given to you; seek and you will find; knock and the door will be opened to you. For everyone who asks receives; he who seeks finds; and to him who knocks, the door will be opened.

It sounds incredibly clear, doesn't it? Yet, I've found that receiving answers to prayer is much more complicated and indefinable than that. It seems every time I've knocked, the door down the hall has opened, and I'm left standing there saying, "Is that for me?"

But I had a new thought the other day; I've done a lot of asking, seeking, and knocking in my spiritual growth, and although the way has been hard sometimes, I've always received answers. Why is it we usually read that passage in Matthew as being completely literal? Certainly God does answer our prayers for material things. But mention is rarely made of how God wants us to ask, seek, and knock with all our hearts in order to grow into a rich and close relationship with Him. Maybe that's why we don't get everything material we ask for, so we actually have a need to hunger after God.

Why are answers to prayer such a stumbling block in our relationship to God? Why is it that people will say, "God never did anything for me," and use that as an excuse not to get to know Him better?

I mentioned at the beginning how God had answered my prayer for a boyfriend—a typically juvenile type of prayer. For a while I was spiritually high from that experience. But then, something else came up in my life that I needed an answer to. So, I sat down with the same Bible texts I had used before and tried to repeat my success. It was a dismal failure, and I was discouraged. What had happened? I was doing everything right!

I think the Lord purposely "changes the rules" on us, that He allows us to make mistakes and have failures in our prayers so that we will be challenged to approach closer to Him. If we easily discovered a magical formula that could give us the brass ring, then we'd be complacent in our prayers, uninterested in pursuing God any further or learning anything more in our relationship.

If we base our faith on answers to our prayers, we will have no faith at all. Because what happens to faith when a prayer you devoutly believed God would fulfill is not answered? What, then, do we make of our God? This is why I think God makes answers to prayer so difficult to understand, so time-consuming to study, maybe even so painful to experience. "The [whole] point of asking is that you may get to know God better."[1]

Our answers to prayer are precious gifts from God, not something we necessarily deserve, not something we can bargain for, not something we can conjure up with good behavior or even receive by correctly following the ABCs of prayer. Answers to prayer are, in a sense, completely unimportant to God's process of growing our Christian faith. "Now faith is being sure of what we hope for and certain of what we do not see" (Hebrews 11:1). Faith must grow *even in the absence* of anything to support its claim.

Does that do away with the necessity for answers to prayer? Certainly not. But it does change the focus from the *answer* to the *prayer*. Back to my favorite text, "Delight yourself in the Lord and he will give you the desires of your heart" (Psalm 37:4). I discovered that when I really delighted in God, He changed the desires of my heart until they matched His. That solves a whole lot of prayer requests right there!

The first time I met my husband-to-be, I decided that I wanted to marry somebody very much like him. I was too sensible to say, "This is the one," and then be wrong, so I hedged my bets by saying he was definitely the right type. After a brief encounter, we were separated by three thousand miles, unlikely to ever meet again unless he continued the relationship by writing. He didn't.

I was crushed. I had been overjoyed that God had brought into my life a good, eligible (and certainly handsome) Christian man, only to snatch him out of reach. For a while, I continued in a faith relationship with God, trusting Him to work out the situation in His way. I wrote long, impassioned prayers, working through the turmoil in my heart. But, as the weeks went by and the mailbox remained empty, I slowly gave up on God. I was annoyed that He hadn't answered my prayer, my faith slid into despair, and I shrugged Him away.

One year later to the exact hour, I saw my husband-to-be again. Within a few short months, we were engaged and then married. And what had I learned about prayer? Mostly, that I didn't have any staying power. God *had* answered my prayer, but not when I wanted it, so I had discarded Him. It was not the *answer* to prayer that I learned from; it was the *waiting*. During that time of waiting, that time when my heart was impressionable and my soul yearned for comfort, God wanted to teach me more about Himself. He wanted me to draw closer to Him for strength, to cozy up and rest beside Him, to allow Him to show me the next step until finally I was willing for Him to lead completely.

How much more meaningful that answer to prayer would have been for me had I been growing daily with God in the meantime. How I would have treasured the lessons He had taught me when He finally brought about the ultimate answer to my request. God answered my prayer but not because I deserved it or even because I asked for it. It was a gift.

Almost nine years have passed since my husband and I were married. I've learned a lot more about answers to prayer, but mostly, God has taught me how to delight in Him. If someone were to ask me, "When was the last time God answered a prayer of yours?" I would have to reply, "All the time." But it would be an awkward question, because God has changed my focus from asking for things to just wanting to understand Him better.

The closer you come to God, the more you begin to see from His perspective. With that new perspective, it is so much easier to discover answers for the questions you bring to Him. Then you are not tossed about by doubt, wondering if this is the way God wants you to go. If you are making a regular practice of listening for that still, small voice, it will be there when you need answers.

To be so much in contact with God that you never
need to ask Him to show you His will, is to be nearing

the final stage of your discipline in the life of faith. When you are rightly related to God, it is a life of freedom and liberty and delight, you *are* God's will, and all your common-sense decisions are His will for you unless He checks. You decide things in perfect delightful friendship with God, knowing that if your decisions are wrong He will always check; when He checks, stop at once.[2]

The Bible gives us an abundance of passages on answered prayer. Within those promises are clues to receiving answers. These are not magical formulas for success; they are simply some conditions without which answers to prayer cannot occur.

Need
David the psalmist often cried out to God in his darkest moments. "Listen to my cry, for I am in desperate need" (Psalm 142:6). If you don't realize your need, how can God help you? The longer your faith is challenged, the more you understand the depth of your need for God's power in your life and your need to depend on Him in everything.

Often it is when you turn to God for help in a crisis that you realize how much your relationship with Him needs work. So you come, apologetic, asking for some major help but admitting that you've put God pretty far down on your list of priorities. At this point, God has a choice. He can either answer your request and run the risk that you'll say, "Thanks, God, see ya around," and move on without pursuing Him any farther, or He can refuse to answer your request and hope you won't give up on Him completely in despair. Whatever the outcome, we usually give God the blame, not the credit.

Confession
"Dear friends, if our hearts do not condemn us, we have confidence before God and receive from him anything we ask" (1 John 3:21, 22). Have you ever gone to ask God for something and felt your heart condemn you? It says things like, "You

haven't been seeking God regularly," or, "You're carrying a grudge against the neighbors," or, "How do you expect God to get through to you when your mind is full of TV static?"

If our hearts do not condemn us, it is a sign that we have been opening them daily to God for inspection and cleansing. If any of these guidelines to prayer matter more than the others, having a heart free from sin is probably the most important.

It is this aspect of prayer that most people gloss over too quickly. It took me two years to realize that when I approached God in prayer, He was saying, "You can't hear Me because the TV is still on in your head." Asking something of God presumes upon a friendship that has been consistently being built through times of prayer and Bible study. It also presumes a willingness upon the part of the Christian to let God do His work in his or her life, rooting out cherished sins and unholy notions. How can we ask God to do miracles for us when we aren't willing to let Him have complete control of our lives?

This does not mean that God will not hear the desperate cry of a sinner who badly needs His help or that He will tune out your prayers until you can get your act together. It does mean that in order to have consistent confidence in God's ability to answer our prayers, we need to have a consistent and growing relationship with Him with nothing held back.

Motive

Before we ask something of God, we need to check our motives. Often a request that appears good is backed by a selfish desire. What is behind your petition to God? Be honest with yourself. Will it be for His glory or for yours? James 4:3 says, "When you ask, you do not receive, because you ask with wrong motives, that you may spend what you get on your pleasures."

Soon after my husband and I were married, we decided to move closer to his work. The area where we were looking for housing was expensive, and certain parts were not safe. Finding the right apartment was a big hassle. I was growing in my relationship with God and struggling to understand how answers to prayer worked.

So I asked God to help us find an apartment quickly and then graciously added that the time we saved in looking would be used for His purposes.

I laugh now thinking about it, but I was serious. As you can imagine, God didn't miraculously bring an apartment to our notice the next day. And I'm glad He didn't. Because what would I have learned about prayer? That you can bargain with God to get what you want? God didn't want my prayer relationship with Him to be stunted so early in its growth. My motives for my request were totally self-centered, and I needed to learn a lot more.

As you persevere in your petition to God, He will help you to honestly search your heart to discover whether your motives are pure.

Ask

Although asking may seem obvious, often we talk around a problem and don't address it directly. It is much easier to talk *about* prayer than to actually pray. But Jesus tells us to ask and to ask boldly. "Until now you have not asked for anything in my name. Ask and you will receive, and your joy will be complete" (John 16:24). And don't miss this stunningly direct reproach in James 4:2: "You do not have, because you do not ask God."

These texts don't give us permission to drop hints for what we'd like for Christmas; they tell us to walk boldly up to the throne and ask in Jesus' name.

Says Bill Hybels:

> I have to admit I'm often a member of the club whose motto is "When all else fails, pray." Why pray when I can worry? Why pray when I can work myself to death trying to get what I need without help? Why pray when I can go without?[3]

I remember another time when I lost my wallet (yes, this seems to be a regular occurrence). I spent hours looking for it, talking about it, straining to think where I'd left it. Finally, somebody asked me if I'd prayed about it. Embarrassed, I had to answer No. I was too busy taking care of things myself.

Faith

It is this step where many believers stumble. They think their prayers aren't answered because they didn't have enough faith. If the answers to our prayers are based upon the amount of faith we have, then the answers depend upon *us* and not on God. Prayer, then, would be driven by works.

But on the opposite side, most of us have too little faith. If our request isn't granted, we shrug and say, "I didn't think it would happen anyway." What is the balance? James 1:5-8 gives part of the answer.

> If any of you lacks wisdom, he should ask God, who gives generously to all without finding fault, and it will be given to him. But when he asks, he must believe and not doubt, because he who doubts is like a wave of the sea, blown and tossed by the wind. That man should not think he will receive anything from the Lord; he is a double-minded man, unstable in all he does.

When I first heard this text and really understood it, it brought tears to my eyes. Right at that moment in my life I was definitely feeling like a wave being blown by the wind. But is this text saying that if you believe without a shadow of a doubt, you'll get anything you ask for? No, it says if you ask for wisdom, it will be given to you. Wisdom is what Solomon asked for, and he got it in great abundance.

Wisdom is what we're to be asking, seeking, and knocking for. If you have wisdom, you will enter into the mind of God, from where all wisdom flows. With wisdom you will see things God's way, you will receive spiritual understanding and enlightenment, and every action will be a fulfillment of His will. When you think about it, wisdom is the answer to all your requests. What bothers people most about unanswered prayer: that they didn't get what they wanted or *why* they didn't get what they wanted?

The only qualification God puts on receiving this gift is that you not doubt. Because to doubt that God will impart you wisdom is to doubt that there is a God at all.

I hit a snag on the believe-without-a-doubt side of prayer. After my husband and I had been married a few years, we decided to have children. After trying for a few months, it became clear that things weren't going to be as easy as we had thought. It was especially devastating for me, hoping month after month for a baby, only to have my hopes dashed. I had been reading a lot about answers to prayer and hit on the idea that I didn't have enough faith.

So, I decided to clear everything out of my life to show God I had no doubts. I set up the baby cradle; I made plans and calculations. This was the month, I decided. God had promised that if I truly believed, it would be given me.

That was a very exciting time for me. I was mentally prepared to be pregnant, and it was constantly in my thoughts. And then, the horrifying truth became clear—I definitely wasn't pregnant.

It was an awful time for my spiritual life; I didn't know what to do or where to turn. But I took my Bible outside and with tears streaming down my face confessed, "God, I don't understand at all, but I'm not giving up."

God didn't bring me the answer right then, but He did bring me comfort. And although I was trembling inside from spiritual exhaustion, He held me close and soothed my wounds.

I look back now and see how that experience forced me to dig even deeper to understand prayer. God's answer was a resounding "No! This is not how you find answers to prayer." I had made the mistake of thinking that if I had complete faith and did not doubt, God would answer my prayers *the way I wanted them answered*. I was trying to tell God what to do, trying to force His hand.

The Lord took me to the point where I was finally willing to accept His plan for my life, whether or not that plan included children. It was not an easy journey. In fact, I look back on it as one of the most painful times of my life, but I finally learned to leave the form of the answer up to Him. He will always answer, but not always the way you want. Today, I have a beautiful baby daughter, a wonderful undeserved, unworked-for gift from the Lord.

Submission

Although we must believe without a shadow of a doubt that God hears our prayers and will bless us with spiritual wisdom and insight, we must also allow Him to be God—to answer in His time and in His way for our ultimate good. If we have followed the steps of prayer—acknowledged our need, confessed our sins, and asked God to reveal our motives—then we can be assured that He hears us.

> This is the assurance we have in approaching God: that if we ask anything according to his will, he hears us. And if we know that he hears us—whatever we ask—we know that we have what we asked of him (1 John 5:14, 15).

Notice the key words here, *if we ask according to His will.* It takes a long time to learn to pray in His will and truly mean it. It takes long hours of seeking God and delighting in God for who He is. But when you come to the point where you can pray in His will without it just being a rote saying, that is, when your *answers* to prayer can lose their importance and your focus can be on your relationship with Him—with that kind of focus you are not going to want an answer to prayer that would take you outside His will.

> God never leads His children otherwise than they would choose to be led, if they could see the end from the beginning, and discern the glory of the purpose which they are fulfilling as co-workers with Him.[4]

It's not always easy to submit to what's best for you. I remember praying in high school that a certain boy would like me. Well, I knew very well that he wasn't a boy that my mother or God would approve of. I threw that in God's face by saying, "You won't let me have what I want, just because I want it."

So God said, "Fine. Here's what you asked for." I ended up dating that boy for a short time, and was I ever sorry. God had been right, but I wasn't willing to submit to His will.

If you doubt God's ability to run your life and do a good job, then maybe you need to admit that you think you're smarter than He is. It hit me once when I was in despair over some problem that if I couldn't even trust God to fix this little glitch, who did I think He was, anyway?

Perseverance

Once you go forward in faith, claiming God's promises and asking for His will to be done, the next step is perseverance. Now you are dealing with "things unseen." Today's society is built upon the idea of instant gratification: a few short hours will take you across the Atlantic; microwaves warm up entire dinners in minutes; faxes bring us documents in seconds.

God's ways are sure—but in His timing. There is sometimes a lag between the "unseen" and the "seen." That is for faith to handle. Perseverance is what causes us to grow as Christians.

Obedience

As we grow in our relationship with God, we prove that our love is real by following what He asks of us. Ultimately, when the answer to our request comes, we may find it somewhat different from what we expected and discover we need to do something we hadn't planned on doing. God requires absolute obedience as a sign that we have given our entire lives over to His guidance.

If you don't respond to what He tells you to do, He may stop speaking to you until you get things right with Him. What God asks may not always make sense; remember we're still dealing with "things unseen." If you're a parent, you know that you often ask your children to do things that don't make sense to them, either.

Some of the most important decisions in my life have made no sense at all from a worldly perspective. But I have learned that I can't afford not to respond to his [the Spirit's] leadings. So if God tells you to do something, do it! Trust him! Take the risk![5]

Thanksgiving

"Enter his gates with thanksgiving and his courts with praise; give thanks to him and praise his name" (Psalm 100:4). Acknowledging our blessings makes our hearts swell with praise to God. And if we praise God for His answers to prayer even before they are realized, we illustrate our faith in His care for us.

God is waiting for you to ask, seek, and knock after Him. "Seek the Lord while he may be found; call on him while he is near" (Isaiah 55:6).

Prayer: Lord, help me to remember to seek after You and not the answers to my requests. Give me the strength to wait for Your answers in Your time.

Practice: Make an "Answers to Prayer" box for your family. Place the box in a prominent place. Every few months, open the box and read about God's gifts to you.

---

1. Oswald Chambers, *My Utmost for His Highest*, 57.
2. Ibid.
3. Bill Hybels, *Too Busy Not to Pray*, 88.
4. Ellen G. White, *The Desire of Ages*, 224, 225.
5. Hybels, 126.

Chapter 9

Finding the Center

"Pray continually." Two words. Straightforward and commanding. No *ifs* or *buts*, no qualifiers accompany them. The sentence is complete; the message clear: Pray all the time. There is no room for argument or interpretation, no theological adjustments, no disclaimers. Pray without ceasing. Never stop praying (see 1 Thessalonians 5:17).

How often do you hear continuous prayer talked about, preached on, or practiced? Is it even possible? Are we talking about something that's merely symbolic, a pleasing attitude, instead of a literal Christian standard? Certainly no one has time in his or her day to pray continuously. Paul couldn't have been talking about a hard, solid reality!

It might be easy to dismiss this verse with some clever mental gymnastics, except for the fact that there are some Christians who actually put it into practice. They must be monks, you say, locked away in a cold, dark monastery on their knees all day. Well, yes, one of them was a monk, but he actually tried to spend *less* time in formal prayer than the monastery would allow.

Brother Lawrence, a Carmelite monk in the 1600s, was assigned to work in the kitchen—a job he did not enjoy. But day by day, month by month, he practiced the art of the Presence of God until every single action that he performed was done as a prayer to God. He says:

> The time of business . . . does not with me differ from
> the time of prayer, and in the noise and clatter of my

kitchen, while several persons are at the same time calling for different things, I possess God in as great tranquillity as if I were upon my knees at the blessed sacrament.[1]

Brother Lawrence considered God as the beginning and ending of all his thoughts. There wasn't any activity that wasn't worthy of being done as an act of love for God. He did not distinguish between his formal times of praying and his times of business, because he was continually practicing God's presence.

Prayer of this kind puts God in the center of your life like the hub of a wagon wheel. Everything you do, then, radiates outward from this center. God, as Creator, is the Center of the universe, the Being around whom the galaxies revolve. But He cannot force His way into the center of your life. Only you can invite Him there and keep Him there through constant practice—praying continually. John 15:4 reminds us to "remain in me, and I will remain in you."

Let me illustrate it this way. When my husband finished seminary, we returned to two small churches in our conference. We were far from family and friends, and our small town had no employment to offer me. It was during this "quiet" time in my life that God really led me deep into an intimate prayer experience with Him. With no distractions of a job or children, I was able to concentrate completely on the lessons He had prepared for me.

It was a hard two years, but I emerged from it with a faith made solid by God's testing. Previously, any troubles I experienced would completely knock away my faith in God. But after those two years, I was able to say that "in all things God works for the good of those who love him" (Romans 8:28).

Then tragedy struck our family. My husband's father was diagnosed with a grade-four astrocytoma brain tumor and given only a few months to live. My husband and his three brothers all decided they wanted to be near home for Dad's remaining time. Through a wonderful answer to prayer, my husband was called to be a youth pastor at a church very near his parents' home, and soon we were moving.

But until my husband and I and his other married brother could finalize on buying houses, we all crammed into Mom and Dad's house. There were three married couples and two single guys, five cats, and two dogs, all living together under one roof, all dealing with the stress of moving and facing Dad's illness.

Then, to make matters worse, I became pregnant, and morning sickness hit me hard. It was morning-noon-and-night sickness, and it would continue for another six weeks. In the middle of that, my grandmother died, and I had to fly to Oregon for the funeral. I could go on but—I think you get the point.

My spiritual devotions ground to a halt. There was nowhere quiet in the house to get away and meditate, and it was too cold to go outside. I had to concentrate to keep my stomach under control between the stress, the noise, and the strange food smells wafting through the house. I would open my Bible to try to study but could clearly hear every word of any conversation going on downstairs. About that time things would escalate into a confrontation of some kind.

But although my formal times with God had decreased, I was actually spending *more* time with Him in prayer than before. Now I needed His presence with me every minute of the day. I prayed continually, a sort of running commentary on what was happening to me. It was not always phrased in words spoken with mental lips. It was more an entering before a Presence.

I prayed especially for the baby that was being subjected to so much stress. I prayed when my nausea got worse. I prayed when we all rushed to the hospital with Dad at six in the morning. I prayed when I could hear arguing going on downstairs. No, not in a bow-your-head, close-your-eyes kind of prayer, but in a continual conversation with God, a ceaseless coming before His presence with no pretensions, dragging my shattered world along with me and asking for help.

And do you know what? I didn't feel guilty that I wasn't spending quality time with God, my prayer journal and pencil laid out before me, all the distractions neatly packaged and set aside. I was hanging onto sanity with my fingertips, and I knew

God was with me, was supporting me, and was even more real than when I met with Him on a timed and orderly basis.

Eventually things sorted themselves out. It took awhile, though. We moved into our house but spent a lot of time doing some badly needed remodeling before the baby was born. Then the baby came, with the joys and stresses that brings. And then Dad died after a fourteen-month struggle. But I never gave up on God, and God never gave up on me during that entire time.

Now that things have evened out somewhat, I can arrange for quality time with the Lord again. But I learned a whole new prayer concept during that time. I learned how to take God with me wherever I went, to make His presence a part of my life, to include Him in my inner conversations. I learned how to put God in the center and hold onto that quiet place when everything else around me was in turmoil.

Most of us divide up our lives like a pie: One slice is for family, one slice for work, one slice for personal growth, and one slice for God. But putting God in the center completely changes the focus of our lives; He is no longer a part but the source.

Sue Monk Kidd chronicles her journey to put God in the center in her book *God's Joyful Surprise*.

> We are called to live a life rich and full, but rooted firmly in the center where all is drawn together in God and then flows out of His presence. That is when life becomes the silent dance revolving around Him, alive with the music of His love.[2]

When you are drawn into a life-changing relationship with God, when He begins to reveal Himself to you in startling glimpses and illusive visions, the tendency on your part is to want to take Him with you into the desert, there to meditate on Him more fully without the distractions of daily living. This is the way those called to full-time ministry often live—the monks or nuns cloistering themselves in solitude, alone with God. There is nothing wrong with wanting to be so completely focused on God, to eat and drink Him to the fullest. But very few of us are given that rare opportunity to solely pursue God outside of mainstream society, and even if we are, it is often only temporarily.

Author Ernest Boyer, Jr., chaplain at Youville Hospital in Cambridge, Massachusetts, writes of his feelings of longing when he heard a seminar speaker extolling the virtues of spirituality in the desert. After the lecture, he approached the speaker and asked, "Just one question. Is there child care in the desert?"

Despite that innate longing to be totally alone with God, to be swallowed up in intimacy with Him, most of us will never have that luxury. We are called to leave the mountaintop where we have met with God and return to the valley to take up the threads of our varied lives. Boyer calls these two differing approaches to God "the spirituality of life at the edge" and "the spirituality of life at the center."

Life at the edge "is a craving for the transcendent so single-minded that it comes to consider everything else—even comfort, companionship, and peace of mind—unimportant."[3] It is a life such as John the Baptist led.

"Life at the center," however, "lives the reality of the presence of God in the now of every moment of every act that is done. It is a life that sees the greatness of the smallest of tasks, since these, as all others, are of God's work."[4] This was the kind of "practicing the presence of God" that Brother Lawrence discovered working in his kitchen. This is the presence of God you can discover working in yours.

If you have God as your constant companion, if He is continually in your thoughts and conversations, then every movement and every task that you perform becomes a prayerful act of worship to Him. Your entire day is transformed, your entire routine is elevated as it is performed in adoration for Him. All this without one step into the desert.

It is a wonderful experience to start the day with God in prayer. But something is off center if we walk out of our prayer closet and shut the door on Him, if we leave Him there until tomorrow. Bringing God with us during the day requires practice and patience—the development of the art of praying continually.

Loving glances

Sue Monk Kidd describes one day when her young daughter ran into the room and looked her over intently. "What do you want?" she asked.

"Nothing," replied the daughter. "I just wanted to see you."

Prayer helps us to stop and look intently at God, to recognize that He is there, and to reinvite Him into our lives. Throughout the day we need to stop, take a deep breath, refocus, and put God back in the center where He belongs. It is a sad commentary on our lives that most of us are too busy to take time to think about God, much less to make Him a daily companion. If you can't find time for God in your day, think carefully and prayerfully about what you might eliminate to give God room.

During the day, whenever you realize that your thoughts are far from God, don't castigate yourself for your inattention; just stop and take a loving glance at God, inviting Him back to the center.

Continuous dialogue

When I was little, I often made up stories to amuse myself. Sometimes I was a princess; sometimes I had been captured by Indians. Whatever the story, it followed me throughout the day. I would take up the thread of the story whenever I had a few minutes of quiet time or was engaged in an activity in which I didn't have to concentrate. Sometimes the story would continue over several days until it finally either came to a dramatic conclusion or I lost interest in it.

Now that I'm an adult, I don't make up stories. But I do have an activity that engages my mind when I have a few minutes of quiet. It's called worry. No matter how busy I am, if there is something really bothering me, I always manage to find the time to think about it.

If we can allow worry to form the backdrop of our thoughts, why not God? Isn't He a much more worthy topic of thought than how to pay the bills or Indian-slave-girl stories? The key is to learn how to make thoughts of God thread continuously through our minds.

If you decide to bring God with you when you leave your prayer room, then imagine that He is with you all the time. Whatever you are doing, talk to Him about it. Hold a running conversation with Him. Consult Him about the new shoes you are buying, the contract you are drawing up, the potatoes you are peeling. When your mind is free, continue the conversation in detail. Tell Him about your worries, the angry thoughts you have, the joy a fresh morning brings you. The more you practice dialoguing with God, the more aware of Him you will be. And you will soon begin to hear His voice in your life more clearly.

If you momentarily forget God in your business, just pick up the thread of your conversation again, and continue on in your fellowship. Make Him a part of *everything* you do.

Association

It is inevitable that we will eventually forget God at some time during the day. An easy way to remind yourself to return to Him in your thoughts is to associate God with routine happenings of the day.

For example, every day on your way to work you pass a beautiful cottage landscaped with bright and cheery flowers. You always notice that house because it is so pretty. Make that house a landmark for God. When you see that house each morning, connect it with God so that your thoughts will naturally turn to Him.

Snatching tiny moments

Our days are filled with tiny moments of waiting that go unnoticed or are filled with worry or meaningless chatter. Seize these moments and dedicate them to God. You can find them anywhere—the time you wait at a red light. The time you spend on hold on the phone. The time you spend waiting for the shower water to heat up. These moments are everywhere; take advantage of them.

Before you begin an activity, take a moment to consecrate

that activity to God, and when you finish, offer it up to Him as a gift of love. Those few seconds change an ordinary routine into wondrous worship.

Repetitious prayer

Another way to put God in the center is to practice repeating a prayer of invitation. The story is told of a pilgrim who had experienced much hardship in his life. After his wife died suddenly, he began to wander with his Bible, seeking solace. Stumbling upon Paul's words to pray without ceasing, he sought relentlessly to discover how to accomplish this. Eventually, he was introduced to a form of repetitious prayer. He practiced praying the one line, "Lord Jesus Christ, have mercy on me," continually. He says:

> I got so accustomed to the prayer of the heart that I practiced it without ceasing and finally I felt that the Prayer of itself, without any effort on my part, began to function both in my mind and heart. . . . My soul praised God and my heart overflowed with joy.[5]

Although this may seem strange at first, it becomes more comfortable with use. Other short prayers might be, "Lord Jesus Christ, dwell in me," or merely repeating the name of God or Jesus over and over. I personally like the Hebrew form of Jesus—Yeshua. It has such a soft, poetic sound.

You can spend quiet time apart just meditating on your short prayer and then slowly learn how to integrate it into the current of your daily routine. Practice consciously saying those words over and over as you go about your activities until they become associated with and as natural as breathing.

Eventually a prayer like that becomes part of you; it is something that you are no longer consciously repeating, but is being replayed in your subconscious. It works on the same order as having a fragment of a song or TV jingle going round and round in your head—only this repetition leads you into the very presence of God.

Prayer walks

The Bible is full of examples of people who found their godly inspiration in nature. King David learned to know God intimately as he tended sheep. Jesus did most of His teaching outdoors, where the people could experience God through His creation.

> As men should lift up their eyes to the hills of God, and behold the wonderful works of His hands, they could learn precious lessons of divine truth. Christ's teachings would be repeated to them in the things of nature.... By communion with God in nature, the mind is uplifted, and the heart finds rest.[6]

If you regularly spend time outdoors, make it a habit to notice what God is saying through His creation. If you normally spend your time indoors, schedule "prayer walks." As you walk, look for God's lessons in the things that you see. You might want to bring a notebook to jot down the ideas you have. Find somewhere to sit and just be "still," watching and waiting to see what God will produce next.

My father tells the story of how he was teaching the Sabbath School lesson to a group of students by a lake near Grand Coulee, Washington. They were continuously being distracted by displays of nature. First, a flock of Canada geese landed on the lake. Then some blue wing teal ducks flew by, their wings making a whistling noise. Next, a Virginia rail appeared, ducking in and out of the reeds. Then they heard the strange call of an American bittern. Finally my father said, "God is teaching the lesson today, and I keep interrupting."

Twenty-four hour prayer retreats

Maybe you can't live in the desert, but you can always take day trips. Sometimes our experience with God needs some refreshing and revitalizing. Although we may be continually seeking Him on a daily basis, taking some special time with Him can help to renew that excitement for His presence.

Designate a day as a prayer retreat. You can do this alone or with a group. Devote the entire day to God as a continual prayer. Spend time in active conversation with Him, listen for answers in His Word, experience Him through parables of nature, and meditate upon the greatness of His character.

Eliminate any distractions by finding a baby sitter and getting out of the house. You might want to go camping or stay in a motel somewhere. Certain religious groups will sometimes let you stay at one of their retreats for a small fee. Don't bring the latest *Reader's Digest* with you or that craft project you haven't had time to finish. Deliberately clear the day and leave it open for godly inspiration.

Seeking after God in this way is not easy. It requires us to live our lives from a completely revamped point of view. It means we list priorities and make decisions based upon them. It means we put God's process of growing us—sanctification—ahead of everything else. It takes practice, determination, and just a little bit of grit.

> Are we prepared for what sanctification will cost? It will cost an intense narrowing of all our interests on earth, and an immense broadening of all our interests in God. . . . It will cost everything that is not of God in us.[7]

Practicing the presence of God, learning to put God in the center, is how we become sanctified. It is structuring our time, even in the demands of a life spent in nurturing others, so that we are marinating in Jesus. The Jesus whom we soak up, who becomes the very marrow of our bones, is then squeezed out into the lives of others.

This, then, is the essence of Christianity; to put God right smack dab in the middle where He belongs and to keep Him there despite whatever worldly turmoil swirls around us. Practicing the presence of God will change you completely, for you will be able to say with Paul, "We have the mind of Christ" (1 Corinthians 2:16).

Prayer: God, become the center for the orbit of my life, the pivotal point around which all things revolve, the center from which all my thoughts and ideas evolve.

Practice: Decide on two ways you will take God with you during the day. For example, talking to God at stop lights, or humming the melody of a religious chorus while you're working.

1. Brother Lawrence, *The Practice of the Presence of God*, 30.
2. Sue Monk Kidd, *God's Joyful Surprise*, 61.
3. Ernest Boyer, Jr., *Finding God at Home* (San Francisco: Harper & Row, 1984), 27.
4. Ibid., 54.
5. Quoted in ibid., 87.
6. Ellen G. White, *The Desire of Ages*, 291.
7. Oswald Chambers, *My Utmost for His Highest*, 28.

Chapter 10

Praying in the End Time

The Lord is preparing His people to stand in the end times. Will you be one of them?

There has been so much speculation about the second coming of Christ, so much date setting, so much hyperbole, that for most people, the second coming is almost a nonissue now. But yet there are many devout Christians who firmly believe the Lord is coming soon. How do they know this?

They know it, not from biblical predictions, not from elaborate charts and timetables, not from calamitous world events. They know it from the still, small voice inside of them.

What does *soon* mean? When my daughter asks for "suppers" and it's not quite time, I tell her, "Soon." *Soon* is flexible, indefinite, vague. I wouldn't presume to put a timetable, even in years, on the Lord's soon coming. But before the Lord makes His actual appearance, two major things will happen: (1) a time of great spiritual fervor and preaching of the gospel and (2) a time of great persecution and trial.

I believe the Lord is preparing His people to stand during these end-time events. I believe that the time to prepare is *now*. Don't be fooled by world peace; don't be fooled by separation of church and state; don't be fooled by how your friends are practicing their religion. After all, the Bible does say that the Lord's coming will be like a "thief in the night." And remember the story of the ten virgins? They went out to meet the bridegroom, but there was a delay—a long delay. When the bridegroom finally came, he startled them all; they'd all fallen asleep. But notice something here. Matthew 25:6 tells of the bridegroom's coming. What woke the virgins was not the bridegroom's arrival but rather a shout saying that the bridegroom was definitely coming. When the five foolish virgins discovered they were out of oil, they rushed off to buy some more. Evidently they thought they still had enough time to buy oil and hurry back in time to meet the bridegroom. But they were wrong—and they were left out in the cold.

We've all heard that story—and the interpretation that the oil represents the Holy Spirit—enough times to yawn when it's mentioned. But the parable makes a disturbing point. Life is good right now. Life is easy; life is smooth. But at some point, something will break into this ordered existence that will signal without a doubt that Jesus is on His way. It will shock us all, devout and uninterested alike. And when that event—that "shout"—happens, totally unexpected and unpredicted, it will be too late to get right with God, to fill up with the Holy Spirit. It will be "what you see is what you get." "Let him who does wrong continue to do wrong; let him who is vile continue to be vile; let him who does right continue to do right; and let him who is holy continue to be holy" (Revelation 22:11).

That is why I believe the Lord is preparing His people now. During the time when I first began growing in my understanding of prayer, I went through what I call a "wilderness experience." After having worked in a very fulfilling job and then going on to finish a master's degree, I did not realize just how much I based my identity on what I had accomplished. Not until we ended up in a small town with no hope of meaningful work for me did I realize just how much my sense of worth revolved around superficial things. It was God's purpose to remove all the other distractions from my life so that I would be forced to face myself and realize how much I needed Him.

Those were dark days for me. On the surface everything seemed just fine. I was living in a nice house, in a quiet country town, with a lovely church congregation and with a great husband. I was even free from the encumbrances of work! But inside, I was in turmoil as I struggled to find a new identity in Christ. I was often depressed and would curl up on my bed to sleep away my problems.

Slowly the Lord cracked through my shell and broke me open, exposing me to the cleansing light of His holiness. It was painful, and it was tough. But for the first time in my life, I was progressing beyond a superficial relationship with God, to a new level I could previously only just begin to imagine.

For some time after we moved to the small town, I had "storm dreams." Each time, the dream was different, but the theme was the same. A major storm was coming; I could see the black thunderclouds hanging ominously in the sky. Sometimes there was a tornado, dark and menacing, advancing straight toward me. I realized I needed to prepare—and prepare quickly—in order to survive the storm. I interpreted these dreams as a reflection of the stress of moving. But yet deep inside I wondered if they might not be giving me a sense of urgency about the future.

As I progressed further in my seeking after God, I felt a gale-force wind trying to blow me back. Many times it seemed that God was nowhere near me, as if He had disappeared, and everything I was doing was for nothing. I felt like giving up in discouragement. I felt that God had made the journey too hard, too difficult, and that it was impossible for a simple Christian like me to understand what He wanted out of all the confusing theories and instructions. One book would suggest approaching God a certain way; another book would advocate a different process. I was somewhat angry at God for not making it easier to find out what He wanted.

Yet when I felt like giving up, I had a strange impression. The impression was that if I gave up now, I'd never get another chance. It was a very frightening, very unnerving feeling. I knew that God was a God of mercy and forgiveness, welcoming us back into His presence over and over again. Yet I couldn't ignore this feeling. More than once I found myself literally clenching my fists and saying to myself, "I'm not giving up. I'm not giving up."

That was almost four years ago. Do I still believe that that was my last chance? I would have to say Yes. Because the Lord has taken me, changed me, taught me, and renewed me so much during these last four years. My relationship with Him has broadened incredibly since then. And it has taken four years to do it. If I hadn't responded to the Spirit's leading then and toughed out the hard truths He was leading me through, I might never have taken the opportunity again. Or, if I had, it might have been too late for God's time schedule. And, as we discovered with my father-in-law, no one knows how long his or her time on this earth will be.

This is my experience. This is what happened to me. What the Holy Spirit is leading you to do only you can know for sure. That it took me four years to learn what I know now might just illustrate a certain density of the brain, or—more likely—a stubbornness of spirit. But sanctification of the heart is definitely not an overnight task.

In any case, if you seek Him with all your heart, you can be sure that the Lord will get you there, on time and prepared. "Being confident of this, that he who began a good work in you will carry it on to completion until the day of Christ Jesus" (Philippians 1:6). "We don't know what perfection is or how to get there, but when we do our part, God is responsible for getting us there."[1]

Since that time, I have met others who were or had been going through their own wilderness experience. The wilderness experience is a time of preparation. It is a time where false pretenses are swept aside and the reality of God's call shines clearly. It is a time of intense longing and searching. A time of testing and refinement.

Those characters who stand out most in the Bible record were prepared through a wilderness experience. Remember Joseph and his years in prison. Think of Moses' flight to the wilderness, where for forty years he prepared to lead the Israelites to their new home. Can you imagine a preparation time of forty years? Yet look at what God accomplished through Moses.

And then there is Elijah and the time he spent hiding by the brook Cherith. Look what the Lord did through him. And look at King David, who grew up toughened by nature and the obstinacy of his sheep.

While still in the womb, John the Baptist was dedicated to the Lord's work. He was literally prepared in the wilderness to perform his brief preparatory function for Jesus. Yet John the Baptist was called the greatest prophet ever to live.

And finally, look at Jesus Himself, who was prepared for thirty years in a simple home as a common laborer. For only three-and-a-half years Jesus ministered to the people—and He changed the world forever.

Although everyone's time in the wilderness will be different, God will use that time to break down all resistance in your heart and lay the foundation for His kingdom. It may be a time when trouble and temptation attack you, when doubts cloud your mind and threaten to cut off your communication with God. Jesus, too, was tempted intensely in the wilderness just prior to His baptism and the start of His ministry. He emerged from the wilderness haggard and exhausted, but victorious.

If you are in the wilderness now, if things around you are dark, let God make the most of that time with you.

> Watch where God puts you into darkness, and when you are there keep your mouth shut. . . . Darkness is the time to listen. Don't talk to other people about it; don't read books to find out the reason of the darkness, but listen and heed. If you talk to other people, you cannot hear what God is saying. When you are in the dark, listen, and God will give you a very precious message for someone else when you get into the light.[2]

At some point in everyone's life, they feel as if Jesus has failed them, as if He is in the tomb. Something happens that casts doubt on everything they were taught, believed in, and hoped for. Suddenly, everything they thought they understood shatters and dissipates into nothingness. And like the disciples, they are left with this fact: Christ is in His tomb. This is the ultimate darkness; this is when evil crowds so close that everything is pitch black and you cannot see your hands folded in prayer in front of your face. The devil laughs and taunts, "Christ is in the tomb." Your heart is breaking; your spirit is in anguish. You cry out to God, and it seems He isn't there.

On the cross, Jesus Himself felt that same anguish just before His broken heart gave out. Crushed under the seemingly unredeemable load of the sins of the world, He encountered something He felt He could not face. His Father was removed from view, invisible in the presence of His antithesis—sin. After a life of continuous communication with His Father, the Son was wrenched with the agonizing separation. He cried out, "Eloi, Eloi, lama sabachthani?" "My God, My God, why hast Thou forsaken Me?"

But God was there. He had not left, and although Jesus had to suffer through the ultimate torture of separation from His Father, the Father, also suffering, would never leave the Son.

> God and His holy angels were beside the cross. The Father was with His Son. Yet His presence was not revealed. . . . And in that dreadful hour Christ was not to be comforted with the Father's presence. He trod the wine press alone, and of the people there was none with Him.[3]

To emerge triumphant from the wilderness, you must go with Christ into the tomb and rise again with Him. "I have been crucified with Christ and I no longer live, but Christ lives in me" (Galatians 2:20). Through His strength you must endure His agony; you must endure the horrible separation from the Father. But although His presence may be concealed, the Father is standing right beside you.

When Christ is in His tomb in your life—hang on. Hold fast to His promises; use the darkness to listen and wait. Stripped of all human accomplishments and vanities, let Him work to your very core. What He asks of you may be difficult. It may go against every natural tendency in your life. You must be willing to give up all your cherished material things, all your greatest aspirations, and even all the people you love the most in your life.

What He asks may seem impossible, but it is the true test. When you find Christ in His tomb, you see clearly what in your life will keep Him there.

One evening when my husband was out visiting, I suddenly had the most frightening premonition that something awful was going to happen to him. I paced the house worrying, and then I began to argue with God. I told Him I could not handle it if my husband was taken from me, that it would be too much. I didn't feel as if God would ask such a thing of me.

I sat down with a book trying to occupy my mind. But something I read triggered a thought. I realized that for all my searching after God, I still put someone before Him; someone else in my life was more important than Him. I had to admit I wasn't willing to choose God over my husband. That was the hardest of trials. It didn't seem possible that God would ask something like that of me. But I realized that if it was in the way of my relationship with Him, then it was an obstacle that must be removed. Finally, with my heart aching with grief, I told the Lord that if my husband was taken from me, I would still be willing to serve Him. The darkness had never seemed closer than during that decision, but once it was made, the burden lifted, and I was able to tremblingly place my faith and confidence in what the Lord would decide. My husband came home a few minutes later, carrying flowers for me.

God brings that point of decision to everyone differently.

> Anyone who loves his father or mother more than me is not worthy of me; anyone who loves his son or daughter more than me is not worthy of me; and anyone who does not take his cross and follow me is not worthy of me. Whoever finds his life will lose it, and whoever loses his life for my sake will find it (Matthew 10:37-39).

Some have had to face the tragic loss of a loved one or the loss of a career or the loss of their own physical health. But from the depths of the tomb comes the resurrection. If you do not let Christ remove that barrier in your heart, no matter how noble it may seem, then you will never find that resurrection—*your* resurrection.

> That resurrection must be part of our lives, visible for all to see. If we have it, we should be able to show it. If we cannot show it, perhaps we never really found it. . . . To live the resurrection that we as Christians have already undergone is to turn all of life into prayer and so turn all that is done, all that is said, into a long litany of praise for God.[4]

End-time requests

So, then, for what shall we pray? In the story of the ten virgins, the oil was the crucial factor. The preparation we're going to need—the cleansing, the insight, the wisdom, the strength—is all given to us through the ministration of the Holy Spirit. We cannot trust ourselves to know what we most need. We must continually follow the urgings of the Spirit.

The longer you seek after God, the more clearly you will hear and understand His voice. It is a process, taken step by step, as you grow and mature and find freedom in His control. But the process has to begin somewhere. Whatever it is that the Spirit is impressing on *your* heart now, ask the Lord to make you willing to make the needed change.

It is easy to argue with the Spirit and tell Him that "everybody else is doing it," or, "I'm really not affected by that." Don't kid yourself. If the Lord sees that it is necessary to convict you on a certain point, then no matter how innocuous the issue might seem, there must be a reason. The longer you rationalize, the longer it will take before you reach the next step in your Christian experience.

Not only should you pray for the Spirit to be in your life, but in the lives of those whom you love, so that they, too, will grow in faith. The disciples were asked by Jesus to pray for Him as intercessors during His time of spiritual agony in Gethsemane. But the devil lulled them to sleep, and they did not fulfill their responsibility. The same symbology is used in the story of the ten virgins who slept, unaware that the end was near. Now is not the time to sleep; now is the time to "watch and pray."

The Bible tell us specifically what we are to pray for in the end times. Revelation, chapters 2 and 3 list the seven churches. Bible scholars have interpreted them to represent time periods between the time of Christ and the end. If that is the case, then we are the last church—Laodicea.

The Laodiceans thought they had it pretty good, that they had a lot of wealth. But Revelation 3:18 says, "I counsel you to buy from me gold refined in the fire, so you can become rich; and white clothes to wear, so you can cover your shameful nakedness; and salve to put on your eyes, so you can see."

Gold is valued for its rarity and its purity as well as its beauty. Gold refined in the fire is especially pure. White clothes, as illustrated in the parable of the wedding feast (Matthew 22), are a symbol of Christ's righteousness. And salve to put on your eyes indicates a spiritual awareness and understanding.

All these things are items we need specifically in the end times: purity, Christ's righteousness, and spiritual understanding. Jesus counsels us further, "Behold, I come like a thief! Blessed is he who stays awake and keeps his clothes with him, so that he may not go naked and be shamefully exposed" (Revelation 16:15).

Now are the days of preparation. Now is the time to acquire the gold, the white raiment, and the eye salve that we need to stand in the end times. We tend to feel no urgency at the moment; we experience no crisis propelling us to make things right with God. Yet the war for every person's soul is being waged with ferocity while we blunder carelessly on through our fast-paced lives.

Ellen White describes this time of preparation in the last chapters of *Early Writings*. She was shown a group of people earnestly agonizing with God for the salvation of their souls.

> Angels of God had charge over His people, and as the poisonous atmosphere of evil angels was pressed around these anxious ones, the heavenly angels were continu-

ally wafting their wings over them to scatter the thick darkness. . . .

Some, I saw, did not participate in this work of agonizing and pleading. They seemed indifferent and careless. They were not resisting the darkness around them, and it shut them in like a thick cloud. The angels of God left these and went to the aid of the earnest, praying ones.[5]

This agonizing of spirit and building of a relationship with Jesus was all being done *prior* to the outpouring of the Holy Spirit and the fall of the latter rain. This seeking after God was being done *now*, during the time in which we live.

Paul says, "Continue to work out your salvation with fear and trembling, for it is God who works in you to will and to act according to his good purpose" (Philippians 2:12, 13).

This is a time of intense persecution for God's followers. We are being persecuted by too much leisure time, by the allure of materialism, by the easy accessibility of spiritual things, by the standard of living we are expected to meet, by the laissez-faire modus operandi of "good, Christian believers," by the fact that Christ has delayed His coming so long.

All of these things interfere with clear spiritual vision, with realizing the urgency of preparation for Christ's return. Prayer is the vehicle that lifts you to the throne above, that provides the avenue heaven uses to transform the darkest thoughts, the deepest secrets—cleansing, mopping, scrubbing, and sweeping until we become a radiant temple of God.

Prayer must be the answer to all the theological squabbles, the social issues, the differences in personal standards. Prayer must be the answer to all the gut-wrenching problems of life, the pain of death and separation, the long-suffering parent, the invalid in agony, the spiritually confused or misled. Prayer *is* the answer, the only answer, to life—to today's world—to the forces that will stop at nothing to take us over.

Prayer is the art of conversation with God, learning to practice the presence of God continually in your life, until the secular and the religious blend into one indistinguishable whole, until your life is performed as a prayer for God, a sweet-smelling incense before the throne.

"He who testifies to these things says, 'Yes, I am coming soon.'

"Amen. Come, Lord Jesus.

"The grace of the Lord Jesus be with God's people. Amen" (Revelation 22:20, 21).

Prayer: Help me to use this opportunity to reacquaint myself with You, Father, to develop the spiritual stamina to survive in troubled times.

Practice: Buy a plant (either for indoors or outdoors) that will remind you of your decision to pursue God. Plant it in a place that will be easily visible.

---

1. Marvin Moore, *The Crisis of the End Time* (Boise, Idaho: Pacific Press, 1992), 60.
2. Oswald Chambers, *My Utmost for His Highest*, 32.
3. Ellen G. White, *The Desire of Ages*, 753, 754.
4. Ernest Boyer, Jr., *Finding God at Home*, 83, 84.
5. Ellen G. White, *Early Writings*, 269, 270.

Supplemental Material

Section 1: Teaching Helps for Small Groups

Introduction

The material in this section can be used as the basis for a group study on prayer. Some possible groups might include:

Prayer-meeting series
Week of Prayer
Small-group Bible study
School classroom
Sabbath School class

The group leader can use materials pertinent to each chapter in planning his or her program. These activities can be selected according to the size and makeup of the group. Some groups will be more interested in discussion, while others will enjoy the group activities. Keep in mind that these ideas are only a resource, not a detailed program outline.

The section **Bible Basics** includes texts relevant to the chapter content. The group leader can read some or all of them—or assign them to group members to read.

Thought Provokers provides discussion questions for the group to toss around.

Group Dynamics is a chance for the group to actively experience some of the lesson concepts. If your group is large, you may need to divide into smaller groups for this section, as noted. Groups of six to twelve work best for some of the activities.

Heart to Heart brings the group together in prayer. This section provides the opportunity for the group to experience various types of prayer formats.

Homework gives everybody a chance to practice some of the concepts at home and to really take prayer with them.

Illustrations are for the group leader to use. He or she can read aloud from the quoted materials to the group or designate someone else to read them. These illustrations from some of the best written material on prayer will often spark discussions of their own.

Supplies lists any items the group leader needs to prepare ahead of time.

Chapter 1

A Torrent of Grace

Supplies

Dictionary, newspaper or poster board, large felt-tip markers, Bible concordance, 3 x 5 cards, markers or pencils, extra Bibles as backups.

Bible Basics

Psalm 37:4	Psalm 111:2
1 Samuel 12:33	Matthew 5:6

Thought Provokers

1. What does it really mean to delight in God? (Use a dictionary to define the word *delight*.)

2. Why should we pray?

3. What do you get from prayer? What does God get from prayer?

Group Dynamics

1. Using a Bible concordance for help, have each person choose a text that will be his or her "mascot" during the prayer journey. On a 3 x 5 card, write the Bible text clearly, and take it home to put up in a prominent place.

2. Have everyone think of excuses for not praying. Write them in felt-tipped pen on a large piece of newsprint or poster

board. Pass the newsprint around. Each person then names one thing that will help him or her to overcome the excuses (for example, "Make prayer a priority") and tears off a piece of the newsprint. Have each person take home a torn piece as a reminder to pray.

Heart to Heart

Explain that tonight's prayer will cover only one topic: discovering prayer. Ask for one-sentence prayers on that topic. Allow time for everyone to pray who wishes to, and close with a one-sentence prayer.

Homework

Share your "mascot" text with one person (other than a group member) this week.

Illustrations

Bill Hybels shares this in *Too Busy Not to Pray*:

Prayer has not always been my strong suit. For many years, even as a senior pastor of a large church, I *knew* more about prayer than I ever *practiced* in my own life. I have a racehorse temperament, and the tugs of self-sufficiency and self-reliance are very real to me. I didn't want to get off the fast track long enough to find out what prayer is all about.

Several years ago the Holy Spirit gave me a leading so direct that I couldn't ignore it, argue against it or disobey it. The leading was to explore, study and practice prayer until I finally understood it. I obeyed that leading. I read fifteen or twenty major books on prayer, some old and some new. I studied almost every passage on prayer in the Bible.

And then I did something absolutely radical: I prayed.

The greatest fulfillment in my prayer life has not been the list of miraculous answers to prayer I have received, although that has been wonderful. The greatest thrill has been the qualitative difference in my relationship with God. And when I started to pray, I didn't know that was going to happen.

God and I used to be rather casually related to one another. We didn't get together and talk very much. Now, however, we get together a lot—not talking on the run, but carrying on substantial, soul-searching conversations every morning for a good chunk of time. I feel as if I've gotten to know God a lot better since I started praying.

If the Holy Spirit is leading you to learn more about prayer, you are about to embark on a wonderful adventure. As you grow in prayer, God will reveal more of himself to you, breathing more of his life into your spirit. Mark my words, that will be the most fulfilling and rewarding part of your experience with prayer, more so even than the answers to prayer you are sure to receive. Fellowship with God, trust, confidence, peace, relief—these are wonderful feelings that will be yours as you learn how to pray.

Reprinted from *Too Busy Not to Pray: Slowing Down to Be With God*, by Bill Hybels, published by InterVarsity Press, 1988, Downer's Grove, Illinois.

Chapter 2

Consider It All Joy

Supplies
   Newspaper, suitcase.
Bible Basics
   1 John 1   2 Chronicles 7:14
   John 16:7
Thought Provokers
   1. What would you wish for if you had three wishes? Why?
   2. Why do you think the Lord allows our "close" feelings to Him to disappear?
   3. Can you think of a Nathanael experience in your life?
Group Dynamics
   1. Illustrate our faith in the unseen by doing a "faith fall."
You will need about seven people. Have six people stand

facing each other in two rows. The people across from each other lock arms by grabbing your own left arm with your right hand and the other person's bent right arm with your left hand. The seventh person stands on a chair or table with his or her back to the row of people. When he is ready, he says, "Falling," and falls backward into the arms of the people below.

Another way to do this is to have someone stand with his back to the designated "catchee," and then, with his body stiff, fall backward into the "catchee's" arms. (The "catchee" needs to be a big, strong person.)

2. Place an open, empty suitcase on a table in the middle of the room. Put a stack of newspapers next to it. Explain that we are starting on a prayer journey, and we need to know what to take with us and what to leave behind. Have each person pick up a piece of newspaper, state what he would take or leave behind, then wad up the paper and throw it into the suitcase or onto the floor, depending on whether it is going or staying.

Heart to Heart

Have the group gather around the suitcase, with everyone placing a hand on it. One or two people can then pray for the group as they begin their prayer journey.

Homework

Using a Bible concordance, do a study on what the Bible says about perseverance. Other possible words to study might be *steadfastness* or *endurance*.

Illustration

In *Mere Christianity*, C. S. Lewis writes:

Now Faith, in the sense in which I am here using the word, is the art of holding on to things your reason has once accepted, in spite of your changing moods. For moods will change, whatever view your reason takes. I know that by experience. Now that I am a Christian I do have moods in which the whole thing looks very improbable: but when I was an atheist I had moods in which Christianity looked terribly probable. This rebellion of your moods against your real self is going to come anyway. That is why Faith is such a necessary virtue: unless you teach your moods "where they get off," you can never be either a sound Christian or even a sound atheist, but just a creature dithering to and fro, with its beliefs really dependent on the weather and the state of its digestion. Consequently one must train the habit of Faith.

The first step is to recognize that fact that your moods change. The next is to make sure that, if you have once accepted Christianity, then some of its main doctrines shall be deliberately held before your mind some time every day. That is why daily prayers and religious reading and churchgoing are necessary parts of the Christian life. We have to be continually reminded of what we believe. Neither this belief nor any other will automatically remain alive in the mind. It must be fed. And as a matter of fact, if you examined a hundred people who had lost their faith in Christianity, I wonder how many of them would turn out to have been reasoned out of it by honest argument? Do not most people simply drift away?

Reprinted from *Mere Christianity,* by C. S. Lewis, published by MacMillan, 1970, New York.

Chapter 3

Still Life

Supplies
A large piece of butcher paper or poster board, crayons, 8 1/2 x 11 sheets of typing paper, pens.

Bible Basics
Psalm 37:10   Psalm 46:10
Zechariah 2:13

Thought Provokers
1. Why do you think God set up the daily sacrifices for the Israelites?

2. What distractions in your life get in the way of prayer?

3. If you had one extra free hour each day, what would you do with it?

Group Dynamics

1. Place a large piece of butcher paper or poster board on a table in the middle of the room. Ask everyone to draw with crayons a symbol of their proposed prayer time with God. For example, a stopwatch with sixty minutes might symbolize an hour of prayer. Or a sunrise might mean praying in the morning. Give everyone a chance to explain their drawings.

2. Give everyone a sheet of typing paper and a pen. Have them draw up a legal document or contract stating how they will set up their prayer time with God. If you have an attorney in the group, have him or her suggest legal terminology, or do your own research, and provide a model for the group to work from. When everyone has written their prayer contracts, have them sign them, and have two witnesses sign, as well. Make these official-looking documents for the group to take home.

Heart to Heart

Set an alarm to ring at the end of a fifteen-minute prayer time. Anyone may pray during this time. Don't be afraid of silence. The basic topic can be asking for strength to fulfill the contracts.

Homework

Set up a place for you to pray. Furnish it with appropriate items, and decide when and how long you will pray.

Illustration

Becky Tirabassi, in *Releasing God's Power*, shares this:

That first morning at home after the convention, without inspirational speakers, great music, or people's faces reminding me of my decision to pray, I walked into my kitchen after sending my son and husband off for the day. A little baffled, I thought: *Well, here I go, my first hour, but where do I start?*

Inexperienced in the classical spiritual disciplines, but not in the gift of gab, I chose to write my prayers. Writing kept me focused, allowing concentration while in conversation with the Lord—much like eye contact intensifies verbal communication—saving me from casual daydreaming and the inevitable distractions of household chores.

Before I sat down, I collected paper and pen and made a fresh pot of coffee. At that very moment, as if God knew exactly what I was about to do, on the radio echoed the regular jingle of the weekly program *Chapel of the Air*. Speaking was Karen Mains, the same woman who two days earlier and five hundred miles away had led the optional workshop on prayer that was *just beginning* to rearrange my daily life. To me, it was *no* coincidence. It was God, in His special and loving way, adding credibility to my decision. He had heard my convention prayer! Now He would be waiting for me.

I turned off the radio, took the phone off the hook, set the alarm on the stove to ring in one hour, and had my first "appointment" with God. Afraid I'd run out of things to say before my hour was up, I talked to God about all I could think of . . . , then opened my Bible to read His words and hear His response. He spoke, and as I listened to His gentle, yet firm voice in Scripture, I recorded in writing what He said to me. I sensed that this was a long overdue appointment, and I was so grateful to be there. When the stove alarm buzzed, I was astonished at how quickly the time had passed and how my spirit was completely refreshed and satisfied.

Reprinted from *Releasing God's Power,* by Becky Tirabassi, published by Oliver Nelson, 1990, Thomas Nelson Publishers, Nashville, Tennessee.

Chapter 4

Dream Stream

Supplies

Praise music that can either be played on a stereo or that can be sung by the group (accompanied by piano, guitar, or whatever else is available), helium balloons for everyone.

Bible Basics

Psalm 34:1   Matthew 6:9-13

Ephesians 5:19, 20   Psalm 66:18, 19

Psalm 100:4   Psalm 20:5

Thought Provokers

1. Can you think of "gray" things in your life? Things that aren't really wrong but don't seem quite right either?

2. Do you think following a prayer format will help or hinder your prayers?

3. Both the ACTS format and the Lord's Prayer start with praise. What is the purpose of beginning a prayer with praise?

Group Dynamics

1. Make a list of praise songs. Sing a couple. If you have a musical group, you might arrange ahead of time for some to bring instruments or for someone to play the piano or organ. If musical talent is scarce, play some praise songs on the stereo for everyone to listen to. If the group is really musical, maybe they can compose their own praise song—some can write the words and others put it to music.

2. Ask each person to find a psalm or portion of a psalm that talks of praise or thanksgiving. Take turns reading them aloud. You might want to intersperse the readings with praise songs.

3. Using one section of the ACTS format, write a prayer to God. Attach the prayer to a helium balloon, and let it go outside. Pray that as the balloon rises toward heaven, so, also, will your heart rise to meet God.

Heart to Heart

Pray the ACTS format together. If the group is small, divide each section up between the participants. For a larger group, begin each section, and allow anyone who wishes to pray to participate before moving to the next section.

Homework

Make a list of the attributes of God (for example, His compassion). Write each attribute on a separate slip of paper, and put the slips into a hat. When you pray, draw one slip out to use during your Adoration section.

Illustration

In *The Cost of Discipleship*, Dietrich Bonhoeffer writes:

This, then, is how you should pray:

"Our Father in heaven, hallowed be your name, your kingdom come, your will be done on earth as it is in heaven. Give us today our daily bread. Forgive us our debts, as we also have forgiven our debtors. And lead us not into temptation, but deliver us from the evil one." Matthew 6:9-13.

Jesus told his disciples not only *how* to pray, but also *what* to pray. The Lord's Prayer is not merely the pattern prayer, it is the way Christians *must* pray. If they pray this prayer, God will certainly hear them. The Lord's Prayer is the quintessence of prayer. A disciple's prayer is founded on and circumscribed by it. Once again Jesus does not leave his disciples in ignorance; he teaches them the Lord's Prayer and so leads them to a clear understanding of prayer.

Reprinted from *The Cost of Discipleship* by Dietrich Bonhoeffer, published by The MacMillan Co., 1972.

Chapter 5

The Wandering-Mind Syndrome

Supplies

Remote control, slips of paper, pens, place to burn paper.

Bible Basics

Mark 12:30   Jeremiah 29:13

Luke 10:38-42

Thought Provokers

1. Why do you think writing a prayer is helpful?

2. What is the method that most helps you to concentrate?

3. Does the idea of meditation in prayer bother you? Why, or why not?

Group Dynamics

1. (Best for groups of six to twelve.) Seat the group in a circle, facing toward a blank wall, chalkboard, or screen. With the remote control, pretend to "turn on" a picture on the wall. This picture is your description of a real or imaginary place where you would like to meet with God. You can describe a place you have been or a place you think would be ideal. When you are finished, hand the remote control to someone else in the group to illustrate their prayer place. Continue until everyone has had an opportunity.

2. Give everyone a piece of paper and a pen. Give them a few moments to write down obstacles and distractions to prayer in their lives. When everyone is finished, have them put their papers in a tin can, take it outside, and burn them. Or burn them in a fireplace or wood stove.

Heart to Heart

Spend ten minutes as a group in silent prayer and meditation. At the end of the ten minutes, allow group members to pray as they feel moved before finishing.

Homework

Begin your own personal prayer journal. Decide how you want to organize it. Buy a special notebook, if necessary.

Illustration

After Jesus said this, he looked toward heaven and prayed:

"Father, the time has come. Glorify your Son, that your Son may glorify you. For you granted him authority over all people that he might give eternal life to all those you have given him. Now this is eternal life: that they may know you, the only true God, and Jesus Christ, whom you have sent. I have brought you glory on earth by completing the work you gave me to do. And now, Father, glorify me in your presence with the glory I had with you before the world began.

"I have revealed you to those whom you gave me out of the

world. They were yours; you gave them to me and they have obeyed your word. Now they know that everything you have given me comes from you. For I gave them the words you gave me and they accepted them. They knew with certainty that I came from you, and they believed that you sent me. I pray for them. I am not praying for the world, but for those you have given me, for they are yours. All I have is yours, and all you have is mine. And glory has come to me through them. I will remain in the world no longer, but they are still in the world, and I am coming to you. Holy Father, protect them by the power of your name—the name you gave me—so that they may be one as we are one. While I was with them, I protected them and kept them safe by that name you gave me. None has been lost except the one doomed to destruction so that Scripture would be fulfilled.

"I am coming to you now, but I say these things while I am still in the world, so that they may have the full measure of my joy within them. I have given them your word and the world has hated them, for they are not of the world any more than I am of the world. My prayer is not that you take them out of the world but that you protect them from the evil one. They are not of the world, even as I am not of it. Sanctify them by the truth; your word is truth. As you sent me into the world, I have sent them into the world. For them I sanctify myself, that they too may be truly sanctified.

"My prayer is not for them alone. I pray also for those who will believe in me through their message, that all of them may be one, Father, just as you are in me and I am in you. May they also be in us so that the world may believe that you have sent me. I have given them the glory that you gave me, that they may be one as we are one: I in them and you in me. May they be brought to complete unity to let the world know that you sent me and have loved them even as you have loved me.

"Father, I want those you have given me to be with me where I am, and to see my glory, the glory you have given me because you loved me before the creation of the world.

"Righteous Father, though the world does not know you, I know you, and they know that you have sent me. I have made you known to them, and will continue to make you known in order that the love you have for me may be in them and that I myself may be in them." John 17.

Chapter 6

Where Two or Three Are Gathered

Supplies
Ingredients for banana splits or fruit salad.

Bible Basics

Matthew 18:19, 20	Acts 4:32
James 5:16	1 Peter 2:17

Thought Provokers

1. Why do you think it's important to pray with others?

2. Can you think of a meaningful time when you prayed with a group?

3. How can you pray in a group with someone you don't like?

Group Dynamics

1. Here is a game to foster group spirit. Limit the group size to ten. Ask everyone to stand in a circle and put both hands in the center of the circle. Now grab hands until everyone has linked up with somebody. Without letting go of hands, see if you can disentangle the knot and get back to a circle. Theoretically, it's possible to get back to either a full circle or two intersecting circles.

2. Try some group hugs (grugs). Stand in a circle, shoulder to shoulder. Have everybody take one step toward the center of the circle.

Cinnamon-roll hug. Stand in a line, everyone holding hands. The first person in the line begins to "roll" up, turning toward the next person and continuing to turn until the group is in a tightly coiled circle with the first person in the middle.

3. To show how everyone contributes to the working of a group, build banana splits or—if you're more health conscious—

make a fruit salad. Arrange ahead of time with group members to each bring an ingredient. Have everyone help to put the food together. The ingredients for a banana split could include bananas, several types of ice cream, whipped cream, chocolate sauce, caramel sauce, nuts, and cherries.

A fruit salad can have different types of fruit, and for some pizazz, add toppings of whipped cream, nuts, raisins, chocolate chips, and coconut.

Discuss how everyone contributes to the whole. Encourage group members to identify themselves with a certain ingredient, and say why.

Heart to Heart

Use the guidelines given in the illustration to pray.

Homework

Read the story of Pentecost in Acts 2. Imagine what it must have been like to have been with the believers. Write a page describing the scene as if you had been there.

Illustration

Evelyn Christenson shares this in *What Happens When Women Pray*:

"Well, I suppose you all know how to pray. I won't fit into this group." With that remark, Betty, my neighbor, joined the three of us meeting in my home to pray for the coming Billy Graham Crusade. There she was, apparently wanting to take part, but scared to death to pray aloud, even with only three other women present. . . .

The rules we applied that morning were the ones our women devised in 1968 to implement our method of praying in one accord. . . . These six rules serve as effective tools to help a prayer group get started, to encourage newcomers, and to motivate timid people to pray aloud. . . .

The first "S" is *Subject by Subject*—praying in one accord about only one subject at a time. As one person prays out loud, the rest pray silently on the same subject, *not planning their own prayers in advance*. This assures complete concentration and fervent prayer on one request at a time. Also, in this way no one is deprived of the privilege of praying for the request before going on to another. . . .

Short Prayers, the second handle, are the secret of the success of small group prayer. Just one, or only a few sentences from each person on each subject allows time for all to pray if they wish. . . .

The Third "S" is *Simple Prayers*. Those who have never prayed before will find it possible to utter one *simple* sentence from the heart when the leaders and other participants avoid using complicated phrases and a special prayer vocabulary. . . .

Handle number four is *Specific Prayer Requests*. Specific requests listed and specific answers noted are a great encouragement to continuing and expanded prayer. Use a notebook or file folder for this. . . .

The next "S" is *Silent Periods*. Silent periods between prayers are a privilege and a blessing. Don't panic when there's a lull—just listen! . . .

Small Groups, the sixth "S," are usually best for newcomers, as well as for the shy or untrained. For some, it would take great courage to stand before a group of 100 people, or even twenty-five people, and raise their voices in prayer for the first time. But in smaller groups they can gain confidence in praying audibly.

Reprinted from *What Happens When Women Pray,* by Evelyn Christenson, published by Victor Books, 1975, SP Publications, Inc., Wheaton, IL 60187.

Chapter 7

Incredible Intercession

Supplies
A book to be used for group prayer requests, a number of small stones, enough for everyone.

Bible Basics

1 Timothy 2:1, 3	Matthew 5:44
1 Samuel 12:23	Romans 8:34

Thought Provokers

1. What do you think happens when you pray for someone? What happens on your part? God's part? His or her part?

2. Could you pray for someone who has persecuted you? Why, or why not?

3. What would you think if you discovered someone was praying regularly for you?

Group Dynamics

1. Set up a prayer-request book for your group. Divide it into sections for Date, Name, Request, Answer, and Date Answered. Someone can make a formal call at each group meeting for requests, or you can leave the book in a central place, and let people write in their own requests. Use the book as a basis for your group prayers.

2. Place a pile of clean, small stones in the middle of the room. Have everyone sit around the pile and pick a stone that reminds them in some way of someone they want to pray for. (Example, a drab rock might symbolize someone who is depressed.) Hold the rock in your hand, and pray silently for that person. Carry the rock with you everywhere you go during the week as a reminder that you are an intercessor for that person.

Heart to Heart

Divide into groups of four to six. Ask each person to mention one name they would like special prayer for, and why. Pray for each name in turn, allowing time for everyone to pray for that person if they want, before moving on to the next name. Allow times of silence for individual prayer.

Homework

Set up your own permanent prayer list on which you place the names of people for whom you want to pray for long-term changes.

Illustration

Roger Morneau shares this story in *Incredible Answers to Prayer*:

On December 1, 1984, I was on the verge of dying in the intensive care unit of the Greater Niagara General Hospital in Niagara Falls, Ontario. I had congestive heart failure and atrial fibrillation that the physicians could not reverse. As the cardiologist stated a few days later, if my wife had taken 20 minutes longer in getting me to the hospital, I would have been dead before arrival. . . .

In the emergency room the staff quickly rigged me up with an oxygen mask, intravenous tubing dripping medication into my system, and a diagnostic monitor to check the activities of my heart. A cardiologist with the assistance of several nurses did everything that they could to keep me alive.

A short while later they placed me in the intensive care unit which was already filled to capacity. Because all the glassed-in chambers were occupied, they assigned me a bed in the open area close to the nurses' station. . . .

While I realized that my condition was critical, I was also aware that a number of other people in the ward were struggling to hold on to life. "This is the house of death," I told myself.

Thirty-six hours passed, and I was still alive and now able to breathe without having the oxygen mask on all the time. My thoughts ascended to God in a melody of praise.

That Sunday evening the intensive care unit was in a state of great urgency, and the head nurse called for additional help to meet the situation. To my immediate right an elderly man appeared on the point of death as two nurses struggled to keep him alive. To my left, a man in his 30s, already having had three heart attacks, stated that he was probably living his last days.

Lights flashed at the nurses' station with increasing frequency as the condition of a great number of patients worsened. Because of my close proximity to the station, I could hear comments that indicated that the condition of some patients was deteriorating and becoming desperate. . . .

Not for myself, but for others, my thoughts ascended to God in prayer. For 39 years I had seen the power of intercessory prayer bring great blessings into the lives of many. . . .

Now I asked for the mighty power of the Holy Spirit of God

to surround everyone with a spiritual atmosphere of light and peace and to restore them to health if it was His will. . . . I had learned through personal experience that intercessory prayers are most effective when I have made sure that sin is not separating the subjects of my prayers from God. I began my privilege of asking for His divine help for my fellow patients. Pointing to the infinite price He had paid at Calvary, I asked Him to forgive everyone's sins.

For a long time it has been my conviction that as Christians we ought to do for others what they cannot or are unwilling to do for themselves—to deal with the sin in their lives. Jesus set the example for us. As He died on the cross, He asked the Father to forgive the sins of those who crucified Him (Luke 23:34). I cannot explain what happens when we ask God to forgive the sins of another, but I have seen the transformations that begin taking place in his or her life. God never violates the free will of anyone, but when we pray for someone else, it permits Him to work in lives with a special power. He unshackles the individual from the chains of sin so that he can use his freedom of choice to choose good. . . .

As I had discovered years before, demonic spirits struggle hard before yielding their prey to the power of the Spirit of God. For about 15 minutes a large number of patients experienced increasing distress, and nurses actually ran to their aid. Then the medical staff's fears became reality as the heart of a Mr. Smith stopped beating.

The emergency beeper at the nursing station went into action, intensifying the sense of urgency. Immediately the head nurse asked over the PA system for all the doctors in the hospital to come and assist. Three physicians raced into the unit. A nurse on the run retrieved the resuscitator that had been left at the opposite end of the room.

About 10 minutes went by while the medical staff did all they could to restore him to life, with no success. In fact, one of them, leaving the room with his head down, came to the nurses' station and said to the nurse there, "The man is gone." Immediately, I appealed to the Lord of life in prayer, asking Him to restore Mr. Smith by the mighty power of the "Spirit of life" in Him (Romans 8:2), that great power that raised Lazarus from the dead. No sooner had I said amen than Mr. Smith regained consciousness and asked why so many people were in his room. He stated that he was extremely hungry, and asked if he could have some food.

Another one of the physicians approached the station and told the nurse to order something from the kitchen, adding, "I have never seen anything like this in all my years."

My prayers had been answered in miraculous ways in that not only was Mr. Smith alive and feeling great, but also the peace of heaven now blessed those present in the intensive care unit. A state of quietness invaded the place. Nurses leisurely stood in the doorways of the glassed-in rooms as their patients actually fell asleep in the peace and comfort previously denied them. As for myself, I could feel the presence of God.

Reprinted from *Incredible Answers to Prayer,* by Roger Morneau, published by Review and Herald Publishing Assn., Hagerstown, MD 21740.

Chapter 8

The Door Will Be Opened

Supplies
Bible concordance, a ball of yarn or string for every ten people, recipe or file boxes and cards for everyone.

Bible Basics
Matthew 7:7, 8	Hebrews 11:1
John 16:24	1 John 3:21, 22
James 4:2	1 John 5:14, 15

Thought Provokers
1. Describe some significant answers to prayer in your life.

Describe some significant failures. What did you learn from both?

2. Do you think you're smarter than God? Why, or why not?

3. How can we live in the "unseen" of faith while waiting for the "seen"?

Group Dynamics

1. Use a Bible concordance to look up texts on prayer. Do you see any patterns? Write down the basic principles of prayer.

2. Play the string game. Have everyone sit in a circle. The first person states a request he or she has of God. Then, while holding the end of the string, he then tosses the string ball to another member of the group. That person makes a request and tosses the ball to another person. Keep going until everyone has had a turn. You should have a spider's web of requests connecting the group. Now unwind the web. Each person says one thing he or she is thankful to God for as he returns the string ball to the person before him.

3. Make an answered-prayer box. If there are too many people in your group to supply them all with boxes, then give them all several file or recipe cards to start with, and they can buy their own boxes. On each card, write an answer to prayer you have had, and put the date on it. Collect these cards in a pretty box. As you experience answers to prayer, add them to the box. Periodically review your prayer answers. This is especially nice to use for families, where everyone can add a card to the box.

Heart to Heart

Pray for wisdom in understanding how answers to prayer work. Claim James 1:5-8.

Homework

Make a family prayer-request book or an answered-prayer box. Put the book or box in a centrally located area where everyone can use it.

Illustration

From *The Desire of Ages*:

The news of Christ's return to Cana soon spread throughout Galilee, bringing hope to the suffering and distressed. In

Capernaum the tidings attracted the attention of a Jewish nobleman who was an officer in the king's service. A son of the officer was suffering from what seemed to be an incurable disease. Physicians had given him up to die; but when the father heard of Jesus, he determined to seek help from Him. . . .

On reaching Cana he found a throng surrounding Jesus. With an anxious heart he pressed through to the Saviour's presence. His faith faltered when he saw only a plainly dressed man, dusty and worn with travel. He doubted that this Person could do what he had come to ask of Him; yet he secured an interview with Jesus, told his errand, and besought the Saviour to accompany him to his home. But already his sorrow was known to Jesus. Before the officer had left his home, the Saviour had beheld his affliction.

But He knew also that the father had, in his own mind, made conditions concerning his belief in Jesus. Unless his petition should be granted, he would not receive Him as the Messiah. While the officer waited in an agony of suspense, Jesus said, "Except ye see signs and wonders, ye will not believe. . . ."

He who blessed the nobleman at Capernaum is just as desirous of blessing us. But like the afflicted father, we are often led to seek Jesus by the desire for some earthly good; and upon the granting of our request we rest our confidence in His love. The Saviour longs to give us a greater blessing than we ask; and He delays the answer to our request that He may show us the evil of our own hearts, and our deep need of His grace. He desires us to renounce the selfishness that leads us to seek Him. Confessing our helplessness and bitter need, we are to trust ourselves wholly to His love.

The nobleman wanted to *see* fulfillment of his prayer before he should believe; but he had to accept the word of Jesus that his request was heard and the blessing granted. This lesson we also have to learn. Not because we see or feel that God hears us are we to believe. We are to trust in His promises. When we come to Him in faith, every petition enters the heart of God. When we have asked for His blessing, we should believe that we receive it, and thank Him that we *have* received it. Then we are to go about our duties, assured that the blessing will be realized when we need it most. When we have learned to do this, we shall know that our prayers are answered. God will do for us "exceeding abundantly," "according to the riches of His glory," and "the working of His mighty power." Ephesians 3:20, 16; 1:19.

Reprinted from *The Desire of Ages,* by Ellen G. White, published by Pacific Press, 1940).

Chapter 9

Finding the Center

Supplies

Incense (in a stick you can hold), something to make a circle with—rope or a hula hoop, beanbag or Hacky Sack.

Bible Basics

1 Thessalonians 5:17   John 15:4

1 Corinthians 2:16   Ephesians 2:22

Ephesians 3:14-21

Thought Provokers

1. Is it possible to pray without ceasing?

2. How can you put God in the center of your life? What is there now?

3. Do you think going to work or taking care of a family can be a prayer to God?

Group Dynamics

1. Play a ring-toss game. Set up a circle on the floor. You can use a hula hoop, or you can form string or cord into a circle. Use a beanbag or a Hacky Sack to throw into the circle. Discuss how difficult it is to put God in the center of your life.

2. With one other person, brainstorm ways you can regularly turn your thoughts toward God. Write two ideas on paper.

3. Light a stick of incense. Read Psalm 141:2, and explain how the incense used in the temple services was representative of prayer. Pass the incense to the next person, and have him or her share one of the ways he will try to keep God continually in his heart. Continue around the circle.

Heart to Heart

Pray with the person you brainstormed with. Pray to put God in the center and to learn to pray continually. Pray for each other.

Homework

Practice a repetitious prayer during the week. You might use "Lord Jesus Christ, dwell in me" or one of the names of God, like Jehovah or Yahweh, Jesus or Yeshua.

Illustration

From Brother Lawrence's *The Practice of the Presence of God*:

Being questioned by one of his [Brother Lawrence's] own society (to whom he was obliged to open himself) by what means he had attained such an habitual sense of God, he told him that, since his first coming to the monastery, he had considered God as the end of all his thoughts and desires, as the mark to which they should tend, and in which they should terminate.

That in the beginning of his novitiate he spent the hours appointed for private prayer in thinking of God, so as to convince his mind of, and to impress deeply upon his heart, the divine existence, rather by devout sentiments, and submission to the lights of faith, than by studied reasonings and elaborate meditations. That by this short and sure method he exercised himself in the knowledge and love of God, resolving to use his utmost endeavor to live in a continual sense of His presence, and, if possible, never to forget Him more.

That when he had thus in prayer filled his mind with great sentiments of that infinite Being, he went to his work appointed in the kitchen (for he was cook to the society). There having first considered severally the things his office required, and when and how each thing was to be done, he spent all the intervals of his time, as well before as after his work, in prayer.

That when he began his business, he said to God, with filial trust in Him: *O my God, since Thou art with me, and I must now, in obedience to Thy commands, apply my mind to these outward things, I beseech Thee to grant me the grace to continue in Thy presence; and to this end do Thou prosper me with Thy assistance, receive all my works, and possess all my affections.*

As he proceeded in his work he continued his familiar conversation with his Maker, imploring His grace, and offering to Him all his actions.

When he had finished he examined himself how he had discharged his duty; if he found *well*, he returned thanks to God; if otherwise, he asked pardon, and, without being discouraged, he set his mind right again, and continued his exercise of the *presence* of God as if he had never deviated from it. "Thus," said he, "by rising after my falls, and by frequently renewed acts of faith and love, I am come to a state wherein it would be as difficult for me not to think of God as it was at first to accustom myself to it."

As Brother Lawrence had found such an advantage in walking in the presence of God, it was natural for him to recommend it earnestly to others; but his example was a stronger inducement than any arguments he could propose. His very countenance was edifying, such a sweet and calm devotion appearing in it as could not but affect the beholders. And it was observed that in the greatest hurry of business in the kitchen he still preserved his recollection and heavenly-mindedness. He was never hasty nor loitering, but did each thing in its season, with an even, uninterrupted composure and tranquillity of spirit. "The time of business," said he, "does not with me differ from the time of prayer, and in the noise and clatter of my kitchen, while several persons are at the same time calling for different things, I possess God in as great tranquillity as if I were upon my knees at the blessed sacrament."

Reprinted from *The Practice of the Presence of God: The Best Rule of a Holy Life,* by Brother Lawrence, published by Fleming H. Revell, 1895, New York.

Chapter 10

Praying in the End Time

Supplies

A feather, small candles for everyone, supplies for Communion, Bible concordance.

Bible Basics

Philippians 1:6   Revelation 22:11

Galatians 2:20   Matthew 10:37, 39

Thought Provokers

1. Has the Lord ever asked you to give up anything in your life? Have you done it?

2. Do you think Jesus is coming soon? Why or why not? Does it matter?

3. How can you be sure that it is God talking to you?

Group Dynamics

1. Do a study on the symbol gold. Using a Bible concordance, look up all the references to gold throughout the Bible and see what meaning becomes clear.

2. Reread the section in *Early Writings* in the illustration that describes the angels wafting away the evil darkness with their wings. Hold up a feather and describe a time in your life when you could feel that God had sent His angels to waft the darkness away from you. Pass the feather to someone else in the circle.

3. Perform Communion together as a group. For the ordinance of humility, use basins, or, if possible, go outdoors. Use a nearby stream, river, or lake. Or, if someone has a pool, use that for a beautiful Communion experience. Turn off all the lights except for the lights in the pool. Decorate with floating flowers and candles, and play inspirational music. The group can sit around the edge of the pool and wash each other's feet in the water.

For the symbols of His body and blood, use grape juice and buy Matzah, which is the traditional Jewish unleavened bread used at Passover. You might want to have a light supper with fruit and crackers as well before moving to the Communion. You can decorate by placing tables in the shape of a cross, or, for a smaller group, sit on the floor around candles placed in the shape of a cross. Candles set on mirrors is also a nice effect.

Heart to Heart

Give everyone a small candle. Have one large candle, representing Christ, in the center. Each person lights his or her candle from the Christ candle and prays a prayer dedicating her life to Christ while the others pray silently for her. If the group is small enough, have the other group members pray spontaneously for the person lighting the candle.

Homework

Clear away any distractions. Then sit quietly for at least twenty minutes. Do not formally pray. Sit and meditate on God, and ask Him to show you what you need to do next in your prayer journey.

Illustration

In *Early Writings*, Ellen White says:

I saw some, with strong faith and agonizing cries, pleading with God. Their countenances were pale and marked with deep anxiety, expressive of their internal struggle. Firmness and great earnestness was expressed in their countenances; large drops of perspiration fell from their foreheads. Now and then their faces would light up with the marks of God's approbation, and again the same solemn, earnest, anxious look would settle upon them.

Evil angels crowded around, pressing darkness upon them to shut out Jesus from their view, that their eyes might be drawn to the darkness that surrounded them, and thus they be led to distrust God, and murmur against Him. Their only safety was in keeping their eyes directed upward. Angels of God had charge over His people, and as the poisonous atmosphere of evil angels was pressed around these anxious ones, the heavenly angels were continually wafting their wings over them to scatter the thick darkness.

As the praying ones continued their earnest cries, at times a ray of light from Jesus came to them, to encourage their hearts and light up their countenances. Some, I saw, did not participate in this work of agonizing and pleading. They seemed indifferent and careless. They were not resisting the darkness around them, and it shut them in like a thick cloud. The angels of God left these, and went to the aid of the earnest, praying ones. I saw angels of God hasten to the assistance of all who were struggling with all their power to resist the evil angels, and trying to help themselves by calling upon God with perseverance. But His angels left those who made no effort to help themselves, and I lost sight of them. . . .

Said the angel, "List ye!" Soon I heard a voice like many musical instruments all sounding in perfect strains, sweet and harmonious. It surpassed any music I had ever heard, seeming to be full of mercy, compassion, and elevating, holy joy. It thrilled through my whole being. Said the angel, "Look ye!" My attention was then turned to the company I had seen, who were mightily shaken. I was shown those whom I had before seen weeping and praying in agony of spirit. The company of guardian angels around them had been doubled, and they were clothed with an armor from their head to their feet. They moved in exact order, like a company of soldiers. Their countenances expressed the severe conflict which they had endured, the agonizing struggle they had passed through. Yet their features, marked with severe internal anguish, now shone with the light and glory of heaven. They had obtained the victory, and it called forth from them the deepest gratitude and holy, sacred joy.

Reprinted from *Early Writings* by Ellen G. White, published by Review and Herald Publishing Assn., 1945.

Supplemental Material

Section 2: Teaching Children to Pray

Introduction

Teaching children how to pray has mostly been overlooked. We teach children that they *should* pray, but rarely do we tell them how. Elementary-age children are certainly old enough to understand some prayer basics and to learn how to follow a prayer format. These suggestions can be used for the elementary-school-aged child; you may need to simplify them a bit for kindergarteners.

These lessons can be used for a children's Sabbath School class, Week of Prayer, or Bible class in a school. They can also be used by a parent for family worship. Other suggestions might include devotionals for Pathfinders or summer camp.

The ten chapters from the book are simplified into five lessons: Why Pray? How to Pray, Praying for Others, Answers to Prayer, and Praying Continually. Each lesson starts with a Bible story or biblical passage as an example. Each lesson also has a list of supplies needed for the teacher; **Bible Basics** Bible texts that the children can look up; and **Idea Sparkers**, a group of discussion questions. The **Hands On** activities include ideas that can be done with the whole group, as well as individual assignments. Choose what activities will work the best with your size and age of group. The last section, **Open Hearts**, gives the children an opportunity to pray specifically about the prayer subject they have studied in the lesson.

Lesson 1

Why Pray?

Supplies

Copies of the prayer key for everyone, a plant or plants ready to be repotted.

Prayer Story

These verses come from something Paul said to the people of Corinth. (Teacher's note: Make sure you read it in a simplified version, since the concepts are not easy to understand. The version quoted is the Jerusalem Bible.)

These are the very things that God has revealed to us through the Spirit, for the Spirit reaches the depths of everything, even the depths of God. After all, the depths of a man can only be known by his own spirit, not by any other man, and in the same way the depths of God can only be known by the Spirit of God. Now instead of the spirit of the world, we have received the Spirit that comes from God, to teach us to understand the gifts that he has given us. Therefore we teach, not in the way in which philosophy is taught, but in the way that the Spirit teaches us: we teach spiritual things spiritually. An unspiritual person is one who does not accept anything of the Spirit of God: he sees it all as nonsense; it is beyond his understanding because it can only be understood by means of the Spirit. A spiritual man, on the other hand, is able to judge the value of everything, and his own value is not to be judged by other men. As scripture says: *Who can know the mind of the Lord, so who can teach him?* But we are those who have the *mind of Christ* (1 Corinthians 2:10-16, emphasis mine).

Bible Basics

1 Samuel 12:23	2 Chronicles 7:14
Matthew 5:16	

Idea Sparkers

1. Paul says that only a spiritual person can understand spiritual things. How do you become spiritual?

2. It is the Spirit who teaches us about God. How do you get the Spirit?

3. What is the result of what the Spirit teaches us? (See verse 16, last part.)

4. Do you agree with this sentence: "We pray so that we will know the mind of God"?

Hands On

1. Decode the following sentence from Colossians 4:2 to find out what God says about prayer.

Key:

A B C D E F G H I J K L M N O P Q

26 25 24 23 22 21 20 19 18 17 16 15 14 13 12 11 10

R S T U V W X Y Z

9 8 7 6 5 4 3 2 1

Sentence:

23 22 5 12 7 22 2 12 6 9 8 22 15 5 22 8 7 12 11 9 26 2 22 9

2. Plant a prayer plant. If your group is small enough, you can provide a small plant for each person (cactus or impatiens, for example). A flowering plant is good to illustrate the point. Repot the plant in a decorative container with fresh potting soil. Then water it. This plant will represent prayer. Explain that as we pray, we grow and become stronger and more like what God intends us to be. Plants need both light and water to grow. Jesus says that He is the "light of the world" and that He is the "living water." We need His presence through prayer in order to grow as Christians. If the plant blooms, talk about how we bloom as Christians and produce the "fruits of the Spirit" (Galatians 5:22, 23).

Open Hearts

Ask for three volunteers to pray. Ask them to pray that God will help everyone to understand prayer.

Lesson 2

How to Pray

Supplies

Butcher paper that can be used for a mural, 3 x 5 cards for everyone, materials and instruments to sing some praise songs (piano, guitar, sheet music).

Prayer Story

When you pray, do not be like the hypocrites, for they love to pray standing in the synagogues and on the street corners to be seen by men. I tell you the truth, they have received their reward in full. But when you pray, go into you room, close the door and pray to your Father, who is unseen. Then your Father, who sees what is done in secret, will reward you. And when you pray, do not keep on babbling like pagans, for they think they will be heard because of their many words. Do not be like them, for your Father knows what you need before you ask him.

This is how you should pray:
"Our Father in heaven,
hallowed be your name,
your kingdom come,
your will be done
on earth as it is in heaven.
Give us today our daily bread.
Forgive us our debts,
as we also have forgiven our
debtors.
And lead us not into temptation,
but deliver us from the evil one."

For if you forgive men when they sin against you, your heavenly Father will also forgive you. But if you do not forgive men their sins, your Father will not forgive your sins (Matthew 6:5-15, NIV).

Bible Basics

Ephesians 5:19, 20   Psalm 100:4
Psalm 66:18, 19

Idea Sparkers

1. Why does Jesus say we should forgive other people first when we pray?

2. Why does the Lord's Prayer tell us to pray for bread? Why doesn't it mention something else, like cereal or fruit or cake?

3. Do you have a special place where you can pray? Can you make one?

Hands On

1. Sing some praise songs to God. Some examples are "Alleluia," "God Is So Good," "Sing Hallelujah to the Lord," and the Doxology.

2. Learn the PRAYER PATH: Many Christians use a prayer format that helps them to cover the various aspects of prayer. These four different subjects of prayer are: (1) adoration or praise to God, (2) confession of our sins and asking for protection, (3) thanksgiving to God for His blessings, and (4) asking God for help for ourselves and for others. We can remember them by using this formula:

P = Praise
A = Asking forgiveness for sins
T = Thanksgiving
H = Help for ourselves and others

This PRAYER PATH helps you to remember all the different areas of prayer. We praise God first to help us appreciate His greatness. We ask for our sins to be forgiven so our hearts will be clean and we can hear His voice. We thank Him for all His blessings so that we appreciate all that He has done for us. Finally, we ask for His help for ourselves, our family, our friends, our church, and our community.

Make a mural that shows the PATH. Put the four letters of the path and the words that describe them on the paper, and then decorate it with footprints. Have each class member stand on the paper; then draw around his or her foot. Let them color in their print and write their name in it. The feet can be following a path that leads to a picture of Jesus. Hang the mural in your room so that you can remember how to pray.

3. Give each child a 3 x 5 card. On the card, they need to write the PRAYER PATH and take it with them so they can put it in their room at home as a reminder about how to pray. (For smaller children, make up a card and photocopy it so each one has a copy to take with him or her.)

Open Hearts

Pray the PRAYER PATH together as a class. One child can pray for each section.

Lesson 3

Praying for Others

Supplies

Poster board, paper, and pencils for everyone.

Prayer Story

It was about this time that King Herod arrested some who belonged to the church, intending to persecute them. He had James, the brother of John, put to death with the sword. When he saw that this pleased the Jews, he proceeded to seize Peter also. This happened during the Feast of Unleavened Bread. After arresting him, he put him in prison, handing him over to be guarded by four squads of four soldiers each. Herod intended to bring him out for public trial after the Passover.

So Peter was kept in prison, but the church was earnestly praying to God for him.

The night before Herod was to bring him to trial, Peter was sleeping between two soldiers, bound with two chains, and sentries stood guard at the entrance. Suddenly an angel of the Lord appeared and a light shone in the cell. He struck Peter on the side and woke him up. "Quick, get up!" he said, and the chains fell off Peter's wrists.

Then the angel said to him, "Put on your clothes and sandals." And Peter did so. "Wrap your cloak around you and follow me," the angel told him. Peter followed him out of the prison, but he had no idea that what the angel was doing was really happening; he thought he was seeing a vision.

They passed the first and second guards and came to the iron gate leading to the city. It opened for them by itself, and they went through it. When they had walked the length of one street, suddenly the angel left him.

Then Peter came to himself and said, "Now I know without a doubt that the Lord sent his angel and rescued me from Herod's clutches and from everything the Jewish people were anticipating."

When this had dawned on him, he went to the house of Mary the mother of John, also called Mark, where many people had gathered and were praying. Peter knocked at the outer entrance, and a servant girl named Rhoda came to answer the door. When she recognized Peter's voice, she was so overjoyed she ran back without opening it and exclaimed, "Peter is at the door!"

"You're out of your mind," they told her. When she kept insisting that it was so, they said, "It must be his angel."

But Peter kept on knocking, and when they opened the door and saw him, they were astonished. Peter motioned with his hand for them to be quiet and described how the Lord had brought him out of prison. "Tell James and the brothers about this," he said, and then he left for another place.

In the morning, there was no small commotion among the soldiers as to what had become of Peter. After Herod had a thorough search made for him and did not find him, he cross-examined the guards and ordered that they be executed (Acts 12:1-19, NIV).

Bible Basics

1 Timothy 2:1, 3   Matthew 5:44

1 Samuel 12:23　　　　　Ephesians 6:18

Idea Sparkers

1. Could you pray for someone who was mean to you? Why, or why not?

2. Have you ever prayed for someone? What happened?

3. What happens to you when you pray for someone?

Hands On

1. Make a class prayer-request poster. Put the heading "Our Requests" at the top. Then make lines on which to write the requests. The column titles should be Date, Request, Answer to Prayer, Date Prayer Answered. Allow the children to write their requests on it, and make sure you record their answers to prayer.

2. Think of a person you want to pray for. First, draw a picture of him or her; then draw what you want to pray about. For example, draw a picture of your uncle, and then draw a cigarette with a line through it to symbolize you want to pray that your uncle will stop smoking. With indelible marker, draw a big *P* on the back of your left hand. When you see that *P*, remember to pray for your person.

Open Hearts

As a class, pick someone who needs special prayer. Spend five minutes praying for that person. Let anyone who wants to, pray during that time.

Lesson 4

Answers to Prayer

Supplies

Old magazines, poster board, scissors, glue.

Prayer Story

Once when we were going to the place of prayer, we were met

by a slave girl who had a spirit by which she predicted the future. She earned a great deal of money for her owners by fortune-telling. This girl followed Paul and the rest of us, shouting, "These men are servants of the Most High God, who are telling you the way to be saved." She kept this up for many days. Finally Paul became so troubled that he turned around and said to the spirit, "In the name of Jesus Christ I command you to come out of her!" At that moment the spirit left her.

When the owners of the slave girl realized that their hope of making money was gone, they seized Paul and Silas and dragged them into the marketplace to face the authorities. They brought them before the magistrates and said, "These men are Jews, and are throwing our city into an uproar by advocating customs unlawful for us Romans to accept or practice."

The crowd joined in the attack against Paul and Silas, and the magistrates ordered them to be stripped and beaten. After they had been severely flogged, they were thrown into prison, and the jailer was commanded to guard them carefully. Upon receiving such orders, he put them in the inner cell and fastened their feet in the stocks.

About midnight Paul and Silas were praying and singing hymns to God, and the other prisoners were listening to them. Suddenly there was such a violent earthquake that the foundations of the prison were shaken. At once all the prison doors flew open, and everybody's chains came loose. The jailer woke up, and when he saw the prison doors open, he drew his sword and was about to kill himself because he thought the prisoners had escaped. But Paul shouted, "Don't harm yourself! We are all here!"

The jailer called for lights, rushed in and fell trembling before Paul and Silas. He then brought them out and asked, "Sirs, what must I do to be saved?"

They replied, "Believe in the Lord Jesus, and you will be saved—you and your household." Then they spoke the word of the Lord to him and to all the others in his house. At that hour of the night the jailer took them and washed their wounds; then immediately he and all his family were baptized. The jailer brought them into his house and set a meal before them; he was filled with joy because he had come to believe in God—he and his whole family (Acts 16:16-34, NIV).

Bible Basics

Matthew 7:7, 8	1 John 3:21, 22
John 16:24	1 John 5:14, 15

Idea Sparkers

1. Tell about a time when God answered your prayer.

2. Do you think God wants to answer prayers? Why might He not answer a prayer?

3. Do you think it is possible to pray a good prayer for a wrong reason?

Hands On

1. Write Matthew 7:7-12 in your own words.

2. Make a collage of all the things Jesus cares about. Write the words "Jesus Cares About . . ." at the top of the paper. Using magazines, cut out pictures of things you think Jesus cares about, and paste them in your collage. (This can be done individually on small sheets of paper, or the students can work together in groups on poster board or butcher paper.)

3. Have the students each write a prayer request. Encourage them to think of less-material requests, like wisdom and knowledge of God (but don't discourage material requests). Tie each request onto a helium balloon (or tie several onto one). Take the balloons outside, and pray a dedicatory prayer over them before releasing them. Explain that these requests will eventually fall back to earth, but God will always hear our prayers.

Open Hearts

Read James 1:5-8. Explain that God will give anyone wisdom who asks Him and believes that He will give it. Wisdom from God means that you "have the mind of Christ" and will know what things you should ask for. Pray for wisdom from God. Let each student pray one sentence.

Lesson 5

Praying Continually

Supplies

Small index cards, little pictures of Jesus (if possible).

Prayer Story

It pleased Darius to appoint 120 satraps to rule throughout the kingdom, with three administrators over them, one of whom was Daniel. The satraps were made accountable to them so that the king might not suffer loss. Now Daniel so distinguished himself among the administrators and the satraps by his exceptional qualities that the king planned to set him over the whole kingdom. At this, the administrators and the satraps tried to find grounds for charges against Daniel in his conduct of government affairs, but they were unable to do so. They could find no corruption in him, because he was trustworthy and neither corrupt nor negligent. Finally these men said, "We will never find any basis for charges against this man Daniel unless it has something to do with the law of his God."

So the administrators and the satraps went as a group to the king and said: "O King Darius, live forever! The royal administrators, prefects, satraps, advisers and governors have all agreed that the king should issue an edict and enforce the decree that anyone who prays to any god or man during the next thirty days, except to you, O king, shall be thrown into the lions' den. Now, O king, issue the decree and put it in writing so that it cannot be altered—in accordance with the laws of the Medes and Persians, which cannot be repealed." So King Darius put the decree in writing.

Now when Daniel learned that the decree had been published, he went home to his upstairs room where the windows opened toward Jerusalem. Three times a day he got down on his knees and prayed, giving thanks to his God, just as he had done before.

Then these men went as a group and found Daniel praying and asking God for help. So they went to the king and spoke to him about his royal decree: "Did you not publish a decree that during the next thirty days anyone who prays to any god or man except to you, O king, would be thrown into the lions' den?"

The king answered, "The decree stands—in accordance with the laws of the Medes and Persians, which cannot be repealed."

Then they said to the king, "Daniel, who is one of the exiles from Judah, pays no attention to you, O king, or to the decree you put in writing. He still prays three times a day." When the king heard this, he was greatly distressed; he was determined to rescue Daniel and made every effort until sundown to save him.

Then the men went as a group to the king and said to him, "Remember, O king, that according to the law of the Medes and Persians no decree or edict that the king issues can be changed."

So the king gave the order, and they brought Daniel and threw him into the lions' den. The king said to Daniel, "May your God, whom you serve continually, rescue you!"

A stone was brought and placed over the mouth of the den, and the king sealed it with his own signet ring and with the rings of his nobles, so that Daniel's situation might not be changed. Then the king returned to his palace and spent the night without eating and without any entertainment being brought to him. And he could not sleep.

At the first light of dawn, the king got up and hurried to the lions' den. When he came near the den, he called to Daniel in an anguished voice, "Daniel, servant of the living God, has your God, whom you serve continually, been able to rescue you from the lions?"

Daniel answered, "O king, live forever! My God sent his angel, and he shut the mouths of the lions. They have not hurt me, because I was found innocent in his sight. Nor have I ever done any wrong before you, O king."

The king was overjoyed and gave orders to lift Daniel out of the den. And when Daniel was lifted from the den, no wound was found on him, because he had trusted in his God (Daniel 6:1-23, NIV).

Bible Basics

    1 Thessalonians 5:17   Ephesians 3:16-19
    John 15:4

Idea Sparkers

    1. How can you pray continually?

    2. God wants to be in the center of your life. How can you make room for Him? What's there now?

    3. Daniel prayed continually to his God. What did God do for him?

Hands On

    1. Read the list of ways you can pray continually. Can the class add to the list and think of some more ways to pray continually? Write them on a blackboard where everyone can see them.

    2. As a group, decide on an item or a place in the room that will remind you of prayer. Whenever you look at it, you will pray to God. For example, a nature picture or a plant can be your prayer object (you might use the plant you potted in the first lesson).

    3. Give each person a card. If you can get small pictures or stickers of Jesus, put one in the center of each card. Have each student draw a circle around the picture of Jesus, to show that He is in the center of their lives. Around the circle have them write other things in their lives like family, school, etc. In the center they write two ways that they are going to remember to pray continually.

    4. Make a circle on the floor with a rope or a hula hoop, or draw it with chalk outdoors on cement. Give the kids a chance to toss a beanbag or Hacky Sack into the circle. If it is too easy, have them stand farther back. See how difficult it is to get it in the center. How difficult is it to put Jesus in the center of your life?

Open Hearts

    Divide into groups of two. With your friend, pray that Jesus will help you learn to pray all the time.

List of ways to pray all the time

    Pray when you first wake up.

Pray just before you go to bed.

Pray before every meal.

Pray when you go up the stairs.

Pray while you're riding in the car to school.

Pray when you see something beautiful like a sunset or a flower garden.

Try practicing saying Jesus' name over and over in your mind.

Supplemental Material

Section 3: Leading a Prayer Ministry

Introduction

Once you have become convinced of the power and necessity of prayer, you may find yourself in a position to help others make the same discovery. The following suggestions can help to direct a church or a school on a collective prayer journey. This material will benefit pastors, prayer coordinators, Sabbath School superintendents, and teachers or school principals. Choose from the possibilities presented to tailor your own prayer program.

Prayer support groups

If prayer is going to become important to the people in your church or school, they must be drawn to it by the power of the Holy Spirit. You can help to create such an atmosphere by organizing prayer groups dedicated to praying for the members of your church or school. These prayer groups might include an intercessory group that meets to pray for the needs of the church members or an intercessory group praying specifically for the Holy Spirit to fall upon your congregation. You could also start an intercessory prayer group that prays for your school administration and children, or if your church doesn't have a school, for all the school-age children in the church. This group can be just moms—like the national organization Moms in Touch—or it can be any interested and prayerful church members.

Organization to make prayer effective

A variety of prayer aids and methods can help to put prayer at the center of your church.

Prayer requests for the church. Provide opportunities for members to share their prayer requests. This can be done with a prayer-request book located in the lobby, where anyone with a request can record the date, request, and answer to the request. To allow for privacy, be sure to indicate clearly that recording the name is optional.

Another way to give people a chance to share their prayer requests is by putting prayer request cards in the pew racks. The requests can be placed in the offering plate and then be passed on to an intercessory prayer group.

Smaller churches often ask for prayer requests from the front just prior to the pastoral prayer. Designate someone as secretary to record these requests and answers to prayer as they are shared. Some churches also practice a "garden of prayer," in which members with specific prayer concerns can come forward to the altar during prayer.

Telephone prayer chains also collect prayer requests. Regularly publish the number of the chain leader in the bulletin. When someone has a request, he or she can call the chain leader, who keeps a log of the calls that come in. The chain leader prays for the request and then phones the next person in the chain. This is repeated down the line, with each person praying before calling the next member.

Prayer requests for school. Set up a prayer-request book that kids can write their requests in (you may want to put it in a supervised area such as the school office or library). Make a prayer-request box available for kids to put requests in, and pray for those requests during the school assembly.

Publicity for church. If you want to get people interested in anything, you need to draw their attention to it and make it exciting. Spotlight prayer by regularly running inspirational quotes in the bulletin. Ask your pastor to preach on the subject or to have a prayer-meeting series on prayer. Put up a bulletin board display on prayer. Write articles on prayer for the church newsletter. Interview members on the subject of prayer during the welcome and announcement period. Focus on prayer during the Sabbath School program. All this attention will start people thinking about the subject and wanting more information.

Publicity for school. You could make a prayer bulletin board. Feature prayer in the school newspaper or newsletter. Invite someone to speak during worship on the subject.

Make the most of opportunities at church. No matter what group is meeting, make sure that prayer is a part of it. From the finance committee to the fellowship dinner crew, include prayer in all activities.

Men's and women's prayer breakfasts are often popular. These may meet early in the morning before work and feature a speaker. As their name implies, they can be used for powerful times of prayer and community forming.

Make the most of opportunities at school. Have regular worship each day at the beginning of school. Encourage the teachers to pray at the start of every class.

Why not have a prayer brunch for kids every quarter? Plan an easy breakfast menu that the faculty can provide. Invite the kids to come before school starts. Have a sign-up sheet so that you can plan on a certain number. Include a special speaker, music, and prayer in your prayer breakfast.

Encourage individual prayer at church. Encourage your members to become active in their own personal devotions and to make prayer a priority in their lives. You might make up a special bulletin insert that inspires people to pray.

Provide prayer groups that members can join. Encourage them to find prayer partners to strengthen their prayer muscle.

Encourage individual prayer at school. Form an intercessory prayer group for kids. Have them pray for the requests in the prayer book or prayer box, as well as other requests they may know of. They can meet once a week or twice a month during lunch, recess, or Bible class.

Encourage students to pray together. Just as they have "swim buddies," encourage them to find "prayer buddies." Provide time for them to pray as a group and in twos.

Special times of prayer

Sometimes it is important to take time out and really focus

on the subject of prayer. These intense and prayerful times can be the highlight of your prayer program, the source for volunteers, and the impetus for future prayer programs.

Workshops and seminars at church. Depending on your church's budget, you can invite a guest speaker to speak for a weekend seminar or special workshop. If you can't afford to fly someone in, seek prayerfully for someone nearby who is knowledgeable on the subject. You might have a guest speak for church and do a couple of other programs on Friday evening and Sabbath afternoon.

A day-long prayer workshop will cram a lot of information into a short time. Offer several different options in the morning and afternoon with a hearty lunch sandwiched in the middle. Close with a prayer-oriented inspirational meeting.

Workshops and seminars at school. Plan a Week of Prayer on prayer. Provide a guest speaker, or set up various prayer classes the kids can attend. Spend lots of time in formal prayer, as well as in musical prayer praise.

Prayer retreats for the church. If you have a group who has truly become interested in pursuing the mystery of prayer, plan a prayer retreat. You can go to a retreat center near you for a couple of days or make it a day-long affair at a local park. Allow times for group prayer and individual prayer and meditation.

Being in nature can be a prayer in itself. Use your prayer retreats as times to hear God's voice in His creation. Try sponsoring a prayer walk on a Sabbath afternoon. Pick a beautiful nature trail, and stop periodically to thank God for something you find in nature.

Prayer retreats for the school. Many schools already participate in a Bible camp. Include prayer as an essential component in a retreat such as that, or plan a retreat devoted entirely to learning more about prayer.

Take kids on a prayer walk. Sometimes it's easy to overlook God's voice in what He has created, but when you stop and listen, you can hear Him clearly.

Prayer dedications for the church. At the beginning of summer camp, our staff prayed for all the various areas of camp. We physically moved as a group to each area and prayed a prayer of dedication there.

After the new officers are elected, many churches have a dedication service for them. Try dedicating not only the officers, but the various ministries of the church, praying that they will be blessed with God's guidance during their time of service. This includes more than elders and deacons. Everyone who has a ministry in the church should be included, from the choir to the cradle roll leaders.

Prayer dedication for the school. At the beginning of the school year, consecrate your staff, your children, and your building to God's service. You might want to physically move through the building with the staff, praying for each area. Or invite interested parents to join you (a parents' intercessory group might grow out of this). Even the children can be included in dedicating their school year to God. Each teacher can take his or her class on a tour of the school, praying for the various departments.

Prayer vigils and lock-ins for the church. During times of special need—emergencies or crises within church members' families, within the church congregation itself, or in the community—it is wonderful to rally the entire congregation in an intensive time of prayer. These prayer vigils can occur in response to a need, as in a crisis situation, or be planned in advance in preparation for a series of meetings or a special program.

There are several different ways to run a prayer vigil. You can have everyone sign up for a certain time that he or she will pray. You can designate whether they pray at home or come to the church.

You can open the church for a certain length of time during the day and encourage members to come when they are able.

You can plan formal meeting times during the day, such as before work, during lunch break, and after work, when members can come together as a group and pray together.

Help members to get the most out of a prayer vigil by providing them with specific information to pray about and instructions on how to pray.

Prayer vigil for schools. Many teens have been to a "lock-in" where everyone stays in the school gym or the church overnight. Have a prayer lock-in where the purpose is to pray for a specific need. Again, this can be either in response to a crisis or a planned campaign to support a project or need.

All of these suggestions can help lead people into a prayer fellowship with God. But the most important thing of all is having a group regularly praying for your church and its acceptance of prayer principles. All the best-planned programs in the world will accomplish nothing without the inspiration of the Holy Spirit and His influence in every heart.

Bibliography

Bonhoeffer, Dietrich. *The Cost of Discipleship*. New York: MacMillan, 1972.

Boyer, Ernest, Jr. *Finding God at Home: Family Life as Spiritual Discipline*. San Francisco: Harper & Row, 1988.

Chambers, Oswald. *My Utmost for His Highest*. Uhrichsville, Ohio: Barbour and Co., Inc., 1963.

Christenson, Evelyn. *What Happens When Women Pray*. Wheaton, Ill.: SP Publications, Inc., 1979.

Helleberg, Marilyn Morgan. *God's Best for You*. New York: MacMillan, 1987.

Hybels, Bill. *Too Busy Not to Pray: Slowing Down to Be With God*. Downers Grove, Ill.: InterVarsity Press, 1988.

Kidd, Sue Monk. *God's Joyful Surprise: Finding Yourself Loved*. San Francisco: Harper & Row, 1987.

Lawrence, Brother. *The Practice of the Presence of God*. New York: Fleming H. Revell, 1895.

Lewis, C. S. *Mere Christianity*. New York: MacMillan, 1970.

Moore, Marvin. *Crisis of the End Time: Keeping Your Relationship With Jesus in Earth's Darkest Hour*. Boise, Idaho: Pacific Press, 1992.

Morneau, Roger J. *Incredible Answers to Prayer*. Hagerstown, Md.: Review and Herald, 1990.

Peck, M. Scott. *The Different Drum: Community-Making and Peace*. New York: Simon & Schuster Inc., 1987.

Tirabassi, Becky. *My Partner Prayer Notebook*. Nashville, Tenn.: Thomas Nelson, 1990.

_____. *Releasing God's Power*. Nashville, Tenn.: Thomas

Nelson, 1990.

Unknown Christian, An. *The Kneeling Christian*. Grand Rapids, Mich.: Zondervan, 1945.

Way of the Pilgrim and the Pilgrim Continues His Way, The. Trans. Helen B. Bacovein. Garden City, N.Y.: Doubleday, Image Books, 1978.

White, Ellen G. *The Desire of Ages*. Boise, Idaho: Pacific Press, 1940.

———. *Early Writings*. Hagerstown, Md.: Review and Herald, 1925.

———. *Steps to Christ*. Hagerstown, Md.: Review and Herald, 1908.